Reviewers' Commentaries
(Continued from back cover.)

"These texts were born within a faith community celebrating Holy Week at Grailville for more than twenty years. While deeply liturgical and biblical, they also relate the Christian faith to the needs of our world. Their varied uses — communal or personal — make this book a valuable resource for all who seek to integrate the Christian mystery with the challenges of our human family today."

Eva Fleischner, PH.D. / Grailville

"An unusual, perhaps unique set of prayers. Unusual because (1) the prayers move out from the Eucharist, from the Church's public prayer; (2) they originate in the Holy Week services of a Grail center in Loveland, Ohio, over 20 years; (3) from a group of women profoundly rooted in the Hebrew and Christian Scriptures; (4) asking what God is trying to communicate to us through God's action in our world; (5) prayers recast in such a way that they can be used for individual prayer, for table prayer within the 'family church', for a small faith-sharing group."

Walter J. Burghardt, S.J. / Woodstock Theological Center

BLESSING PRAYERS

*For Personal Meditation
and
Communal Celebration*

BLESSING PRAYERS

For
Personal Meditation
and
Communal Celebration

George B. Wilson, S.J.

CREATED
IN COLLABORATION WITH
GRAILVILLE

T R E E H A U S

TREEHAUS COMMUNICATIONS, INC. • P. O. Box 249 • Loveland, Ohio 45140

Acknowledgement

This work could never even been imagined without the collaboration of:

• The women who served on one — or many! — of the Holy Week planning committees at Grailville over the years: Mary Ellen Camele, Cay Charles, Rosemary Clark, Eva Fleischner, Joy France, Elise Gorges, T. Rose Holdcraft, Catherine Leahy, Lynn Malley, Frances Martin, Joyce Minkler, Elizabeth Robinson, Marian Ronan, Mary Schickel, Audrey Sorrento, Sharon Thomson, Sylvia Verde and the late Eleanor Walker. Exchange and dialogue with them formed the seed-bed within which the images, sounds, ideas, and gestures embodied in these texts were nurtured.

• The Holy Week liturgy participants themselves, women and men deeply imbued with the wealth of our biblical heritage and fully at home with the bodily expression of prayer in sound, sight, and gesture. Their appreciation of the common prayer experiences was the gentle breeze at the cleft in the rock, whispering, "What if . . . ?"

• Nancy Hennessey Cooney who, after I had tiptoed around the idea of such a work for years, became the catalyst for the first major steps beyond dreaming and into action. Somebody has to say, "We're going to make this happen." Nancy was that somebody.

• Jerry Pottebaum, whose name "happened to" pop up in a brainstorming session with Audrey Sorrento. Besides emerging as a very wise and helpful editor and publisher, he led me (a most willing accomplice) into the best sessions of trading post-Vatican II war stories I've had in years. As Frank Skeffington says on his deathbed in *The Last Hurrah*, "How do you thank someone for a million laughs?"

To one and all, my deep thanks and appreciation. The book can't possibly do justice to the life and lives which gave it birth, but it is my hope that in some way it may nurture similar experience in you as you and your community pray along with it.

George B. Wilson, S.J.

Cover & Illustrations by Julie Lonneman.

Contents

INTRODUCTION

BLESSING PRAYERS

Blessing — benediction — eucharist — Eucharist.

These prayers are grounded in the conviction that there must be a seamless connector, an unbroken thread, between the individual Christian's life of personal prayer and the public liturgy, the Eucharist, of the Christian community. Granted, the action of the Eucharist, as the culmination of the church's sacramental reality, is an action of a different order than personal prayer. But if it is not only different from but also not grounded in the blessing-life of the community's individual members, it risks becoming that most counterfeit of all realities, a dead sacrament.

These prayers had their origin in the Holy Week services of a small Christian community. A word about their genesis will serve to highlight further convictions on which they are founded.

The community in question has gathered each Holy Week for over 20 years, at one of the centers run by the Grail movement, in Loveland, Ohio. Each year a small group would gather early in the year to reflect on the ways we were experiencing the action of God in our world, personally and collectively. We asked ourselves the questions: *How is what is taking place in our world moving and affecting us? Where is God in all this? What is God trying to communicate to us? What light does the mystery of Jesus have to shed on these experiences — and how do they lead us into new questions about the Jesus we thought we knew? What form does our blessing of our God need to take in light of these events?*

A second conviction easily discloses itself within these questions. It is the faith that our secular world is not some irrelevant play-thing tossed out into space and left on its own by a whimsical god, but rather the arena in which the reality and intentions of God are disclosed and made accessible to us. The events of civic, public, national, and international life — its excesses as well as its hard-earned wisdom — are the stuff of God's continuing self-disclosure and self-communication. To desire to contact the all-holy One while denigrating the importance of realities which stir deep movements within our human spirits is to risk some sort of gnostic, anti-incarnational quest for transcendence. It is ultimately to deny the meaning of Jesus. An a-historical Eucharist should be a contradiction in terms.

The women who reflected on their experience in order to discover what we might be called to pray about each Holy Week were also deeply grounded in the riches of the Hebrew and Christian scriptures. And thus another conviction. Christian prayer, while arising out of the contemporary experience of the journey of life, finds its finest expression in the heritage of a people stretching back to the origins of creation, handed down in the holy writings we call sacred scripture. You will find in these prayers recurring evocations of ancestors who live within our psyches, of the events in which they encountered God, and the meaning they have wrestled from those events. The Christian community at worship is not some cocoon concocting fleeting wisps of meaning out of its own puny experience in isolation from the immense work of God, it is one cell of a life-stream fed by generations of men and women who have wrestled with angels and demons in the search for wisdom.

One aspect of the Holy Week experience that cannot be communicated by the prayers in this collection is that of the ritual which accompanied their initial proclamation. The community that prayed these prayers appreciates the power of ritual: body, sight, sound, smell, music, environment, and gesture were not merely 'accompaniment' but rather integral to the prayer experience. In prayer as in every human activity we are body-persons, not simply minds — or even only spirits. As you pray these prayers in the absence of the rituals which originally incarnated them, I encourage you to attend to the physical settings, sounds, smells and body gestures which might make the words have fuller life for you.

How did we get from the liturgical, Eucharistic settings for which these prayers were composed to their form as presented in this book? Once again, through experience. Participants at these liturgies frequently commented that the oral event of hearing the texts 'on the fly' was rich and deeply nourishing but it left them with the desire to return to the words in a more personal setting, where they could stop at a word or a phrase and let it have its own life within them. Gradually the idea took hold that this work could enrich a wider audience.

But only as formal Eucharistic prayers? That notion was too restrictive, besides running counter to the first conviction named above. If the prayer form used in the liturgy becomes some sort of formula so stylized and set apart that it would not enter into the consciousness of an individual Christian to use it for personal prayer, the communal has become dangerously separated from the individual. If it is to be genuine, the prayer of blessing must be personally evocative whether it is intoned in a cathedral or whispered in the stillness of one's private space.

With that in mind, and with the help of wise friends, I have re-cast the prayers in such a way that you might use them for your personal prayer, or for table prayer for the family church, or for a small faith-sharing group. On the other hand, they remain close enough to their original form that a leader of formal liturgical prayer will easily be able to make the adjustments needed to make the prayer fit the need of the group to be led.

Forgive me if I offer a perhaps too obvious suggestion for the most fruitful use of the prayers. They have been cast in a sense-line format so that the visual layout itself will invite you to linger — either in actual time or at least in "mental time" — over the distinct phrases. The hope is that through such an approach you may give your linear mind permission to break its tendency to rush along to the next period. Instead, you may allow individual phrases or even words their own power to bring you up short and invite you into a question or a wonder you might never before have formed for yourself. If my formulation leads you to leave the text totally behind and pursue some new personal byway, some new exploration of your own — even to tiptoe into an uncomfortable thicket you had always noted out of the corner of your eye but were never quite ready to risk — why, so much the better. The God who revels in surprise may be playing hide-and-seek with you.

Reading — even poring over — a book is not the same as "being there." But in another sense it may take its place as yet one other form of communion along that unbroken, if meandering, path toward the fullness of Eucharistic blessing. I regret that our contact is only one-way, but if it invites you to share your prayer of blessing with someone else, I will feel rich indeed.

George B. Wilson, S.J.
gbwilson@choice.net

BLESSING PRAYERS

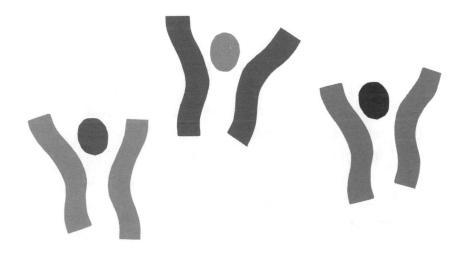

1. LIBERATION FROM SLAVERY

AT THE BEGINNING OF A COMMUNITY MEAL

We celebrate here the fact that our God is a liberating God.
God does not want slaves. God created,
and continues to create,
a people free to make choices,
free to do God's own liberating thing
by being just and caring for one another.

But we celebrate also the way. We celebrate Jesus,
the Anointed one of God, the hope of all the nations.
He is the eminently free one, and he alone frees us.
With us he lived, freely.
For us he entered into death, freely.
In us he continues his freeing mission,
to break the bondage of this groaning creation.

In order to know our God as liberating,
you and I must first know ourselves as captives.

We do not actually wear chains.
That may make our captivities all the more real. No one is more
unfree than the one who lives within the illusion of freedom.

In a small symbolic way let's try to touch the bonds that constrain us.
We want to know our slavery. In your imagination I hand you a cord.
Place it over one hand and pull it to tighten the loop;
then ask a neighbor to tie your hands together in front of you.
Then let us pray for a new experience of Jesus
and his way to liberation.

Meanwhile listen to some voices that may be speaking inside you:

> Who said I am a captive?

> *(Pause. Another voice:)*
> Why am I unable to live with others' freedoms?
> > Why must I forever constrain them?

> *(Pause. Another voice:)*
> How can I become free
> > when I cannot even name my captivities?

> *(Another:)*
> Who are you to ensnare me? Why do I let you do it?

We are to be a people forever in pilgrimage.

> Let us make our way together,
> > for only together will we meet Jesus, our liberator.

Our bonds are symbolic.

But tonight we are one in a special way
>   with sisters and brothers
>   who wear chains we can scarcely imagine.

Let us remember them
and pray with them for liberation — theirs and ours.

Listen and you may hear them whisper to you.

For campesinos in Bolivia and Peru.
For church leaders who speak out against injustice
>   in Kosovo and Central America.
For our American brothers and sisters,
>   voices for the dalits of India
>   and the aborigines of New Guinea.
For those floating forgotten on the South China Sea.
For men and women lost in the maze of our inhuman prisons.
For wives and children battered in extravagant suburban cells.
For those imprisoned within the insanity of the Pentagon.
For the blacks of Soweto and Namibia.

And what are our personal captivities?

We try to name our unfreedoms,
>   the realities which keep us from lives of justice and caring,
>   as a people,
>   or in our own personal situations.

Jesus liberates us
>   by making us into a single caring people,
>   by teaching us to reach beyond ourselves
>   and help remove from our neighbor the shackles of fear
>   and loneliness
>   and ignorance
>   and want.

Paul proclaims the Christian paradox:
>   lo,
>   we who are ourselves unfree
>   liberate others;
>   we who are poor,
>   enrich;
>   we who are dead,
>   give life.

>   As we accept that liberating mission from the Lord
>   and commit ourselves to it
>   in a new way in this new moment,
>   turn in your imagination to a very real neighbor,
>   reach out your bound hands,
>   and silently ask to be freed.

Now let us dine together as a people
>   freed already
>   and yearning ever more to be free.

AFTER THE COMMUNAL MEAL

We have shared together the freeing meal of human communion.
Now let us listen as our Christian community calls us into a deeper
understanding of its full meaning by sharing with us the account of
Jesus' last meal with his beloved friends.

>   The good news of our liberation in Jesus,
>   as told to us by John 13:1-15:

*Before the feast of Passover, Jesus knew that his hour had come
to pass from this world to the Father. He loved his own in the world
and he loved them to the end. The devil had already induced Judas,
son of Simon the Iscariot, to hand him over. So, during supper, fully
aware that the Father had put everything into his power and that he*

had come from God and was returning to God, he rose from supper
and took off his outer garments. He took a towel and tied it around
his waist. Then he poured water into a basin and began to wash the
disciples' feet and dry them with the towel around his waist.

He came to Simon Peter, who said to him, "Master, are you
going to wash my feet?"

Jesus answered and said to him, "What I am doing, you do not
understand now, but you will understand later."

Peter said to him, "You will never wash my feet."

Jesus answered him, "Unless I wash you, you will have no
inheritance with me."

Simon Peter said to him, "Master, then not only my feet, but
my hands and head as well."

Jesus said to him, "Whoever has bathed has no need except to
have his feet washed, for he is clean all over; so you are clean, but not
all." For he knew who would betray him; for this reason, he said,
"Not all of you are clean."

So when he had washed their feet (and) put his garments back
on and reclined at table again, he said to them, "Do you realize what I
have done for you? You call me 'teacher' and 'master,' and rightly so,
for indeed I am. If I, therefore, the master and teacher, have washed
your feet, you ought to wash one another's feet. I have given you a
model to follow, so that as I have done for you, you should also do."

The Word of the Lord.

Lord, we have found joy
         and the disarming of our anxieties
         in the food and drink we have just shared.

Our communion was not profane.
It was the holy sharing
         of a holy people,

rooted in the holiness
of this earth
and of your entire creation.

And yet:
We know that your Son chose to enter,
still more deeply,
into the heart of this creation.
And he willed that we should enter there with him.

And so we bring before you
some of the bread and wine of your creation
— already holy,
destined for transcendence as are we ourselves.
We ask you to labor once more over these gifts,
that they may be transformed into the body and blood of Jesus
so that we who share it
may ourselves be transformed
and become more fully
that same body in this world,
freely worshiping you
through lives of caring and justice.

As we enter into this mystery
we call to mind the waves
of your liberating faithfulness
as time after time
you claimed us out of our self-made captivities.

We were slaves in Egypt
and you summoned us
to be in haste
and move out
in the middle of the night.

We were ready to turn back,
> to trade the hard road of freedom in the desert
> for a return to the security of slavery,
>> and you fed us with manna.

We sold our trust in you
> for political alliances
> and we could no longer sing our songs
>> because we were aliens in Babylon,
> and you delivered us
>> through a good pagan empire-builder.

Each time you took new and strange forms,
> trying to teach us
>> that the way would always be there
>> but it would always involve surprise
>>> and letting go
>>> and risking the belief
>>>> that life is infinitely richer in possibilities
>>>> than we could allow ourselves to imagine.

We sing of all these liberations
> in the words sung by countless thousands
> down through the ages:
>> Holy, holy, holy Lord, God of power and might.
>> Heaven and earth are full of your glory.
>> Hosanna in the highest.
>> Blessed is he who comes in the name of the Lord.
>> Hosanna in the highest.

And so we come to your final word to our world,
> to Jesus.
We remember the stages of his own way.

He watched John baptizing in the Jordan
    and he stepped forward
        to place himself among sinners —
and you proclaimed him your beloved Son.

He wined and dined with prostitutes
    and tax collectors,
    and was rejected by the custodians of sacred tradition.

He set his face steadfastly toward Jerusalem
    and was called mad by his own family.

And finally he sat at table with his friends
    and allowed his own betrayer to give him a kiss.

And when they had sung your praises
    in the songs of his people,
        he rose from table
        and did a new thing.

    He called us no longer slaves but friends.
    He gave us a new commandment,
        to wash each others' feet.

And then he took the bread and wine of the feast
    and said,
        "This is my body given for you,
          my blood poured out for you.
    This is a new and irrevocable commitment,
    reconciling all sin in my flesh.
        you do these things too,
          in memory of me."

Father, this night we join our brothers and sisters
    all around your earth

in celebrating this way you have revealed in him.

We celebrate his living,
his free entry into death,
your gift of his risen life,
and the outpouring of that life upon us, his church.

In the power of his Eucharist
we pray that his Church,
your people,
may be filled with his Spirit.

That we may be freed to care,
freed to live justly
and create just cultures and institutions.

We go forward in the strength that we are not alone.

For we are joined
by that cloud of witnesses
which has been liberated
in earlier times
and now goes on ahead of us
into that land where we will enjoy
the final freedom,
our full empowerment
to worship you in Jesus' name.

Through him, with him, in him
you are blest and praised,
our liberating God,
together in his Spirit,
now and until time is no more.
Amen.

GREETING OF PEACE

This day we are conscious in a special way
of the awful risk in every human gesture:
the kiss becomes an act of betrayal.

As we greet each other in peace tonight, let us do so humbly,
aware of our own weakness, but also with courage,
confident that Jesus will work his peace through us.

May the peace of the Lord Jesus Christ be with you.

AFTER THE PEACE

Lord, we have eaten the food of freedom,
        the body and blood of your Son.
We go on our way strengthened,
        healed
        and grateful.

And singing.

We ask you to stay with us
as we proceed along the way of Jesus Christ,
        your Son and our Lord. Amen.

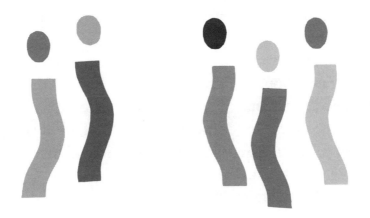

2. WE TAKE OUR PLACE

Our blessing-prayer is always a local, time-bound act.

> We celebrate as who we are — now.
> And where we are situated — here and now.
> And so we need to situate ourselves.

We think of our world:
(These are examples; as you pray, situate your prayer in the contemporary realities where you want to be "placed".)

• We think of the people of Poland, of a people who will not settle for a totalitarian regime but rather heed the call of their heart for freedom and self-determination, pushing against the constraints of their confinement with the power of a 1000 years of shared Christian history. *(Pause briefly.)*

• We think of the people of El Salvador, of the **9,000** who have given their lives because they merely wanted a small piece of this earth to call their own — or perhaps because they are pawns in the obscene power games of others. *(Pause briefly.)*

All: We are part of these people,
              and they of us.
      Through eucharist we want to know this about ourselves
            more deeply.

We think about our nation:
• We think of the poor in our cities and towns; the children
of divided families; unemployed women and men; all those who
will be reported as faceless statistics when the result of government
policies are tallied up — but who are persons with very real,
individual faces. *(Pause briefly.)*

• We think of all people of color, huddled in fear at the awful fate
that threatens their children; watching white men take up guns and
don hideous white masquerade costumes in the name of racial or
even religious purity. *(Pause briefly.)*

All: We are part of these people,
              and they of us.
      Through eucharist we want to know this about ourselves
            more deeply.

We think of our smaller worlds:
• We think of families and friends, people we know,
confronting the mystery of life and death and resurrection
with their own unique mixture of integrity and cowardice,
of anxiety and courage. *(Pause briefly.)*

All: We are part of these people,
              and they of us.
      Through eucharist we want to know this about ourselves
            more deeply.

And we think of our very cosmos:
• We think of men and women being launched skyward on top of

huge rockets, hurtling through space in enormously complex
and expensive machines, landing exactly at pre-selected places on
our earth — raising serious questions about our priorities even as
they expand our vision of the possibilities our creator has placed in
our hands. *(Pause briefly.)*

All: We are part of these people,
                and they of us.
         Through eucharist we want to know this about ourselves
                more deeply.

And we think of ourselves:
• We each look out at all these worlds with our own personal
history, our strengths and weaknesses and foibles — each totally
personal yet never alone, always finding and shaping our own
identity in an eternal exchange with our neighbor and this good
earth, feeding and being fed. *(Pause briefly.)*

All: We are part of one another.
         Through eucharist we want to know this about ourselves
                more deeply.

And we think of Jesus:
• We see him going before us,
                offering himself into the mystery of death,
                shaping us into his very own body
                        by feeding us with his flesh and blood,
                                and so touching the whole of our universe
                        in ways beyond our imagining.

All: We are part of him,
                and he of us.
         Through eucharist we want to know this about ourselves
                more deeply.

Then let us enter into eucharist together:
    the eucharist of shared food
        and shared life,
    the eucharist of shared benediction
        of our common creator
        and redeemer,
    the eucharist of our common passage
        with the cosmic Christ
            through death
            to eternal life.

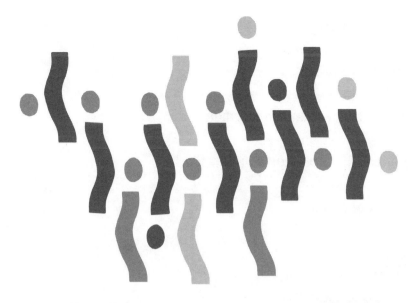

3. CONNECTION AND TRANSFORMATION

INTRODUCTION

It is all really one.
> One mystery.
> One drama.
> One sea.
> One life.
> One womb.
It is all connected.

Oh yes, there is still your world
> and there is mine.
>> Grailville is not El Salvador,
>> nor is it the Pentagon —
>> or the Vatican.

>> Dan is not Carol
>> and Alice is not Elise.

There is difference;
        there are perspectives
        and they are real.

The stars are fewer than the fragments.

There are worlds upon worlds upon worlds.

And yet. It is all connected.

Trouble is,
        we see only the fragments;
        the connections escape us.

Connection is an in-between,
        and that's frightening.

Safer to stay attached to our own poor little fragment.
        Let go of that —
        and you might just fall through one of the holes in the net.

But there *are* no holes. It *is* all connected.

We pray together tonight
        because we have come to believe
        that we are a "we",
        one people.

                We are all connected,
                whether we allow ourselves to know it or not;
                        even when we hug our aloneness to ourselves
                        in self-pity or despair.

                Even when we foolishly try to shut each other out,
                        in childish snubs —

or nuclear confrontations.

Pacifist or nuke-rattler, we are one body,
and we gather to be re-membered.

We are one drama
and we gather to learn our script once again,
to be reminded that we have an audience of one:
a God who takes *delight* in the performance.
In *our* performance.

We are all connected. Then where is the connection?

It is not to be found
in our pains and our hunger and our hurts and deaths.
By themselves these are the crooks and corners
of our *un*connectedness,
the offstage soliloquies,
the stuff for connection.
We are all connected, but not through death.

And surely not through sin.
That age-old parasite clings to all of us
and tries to create the illusion
that we can't live without it,
that it joins and webs and enfolds us.

Sin would have us believe
that it is the very atmosphere that envelopes the body
and holds it in being.

How then? How are we connected?
What is the net,
the center,
the bond?

What lies between?

We listen to Jesus: "And I, if I be lifted up, will draw all things
        to myself."

And we understand:
        It is all connected in *transformation.*

        We are all one because we are all being *transformed.*
                Death and pain are still real,
                        but they are being kneaded into life.

        Folly is stripped and revealed as wisdom,
        and even sin cannot escape the gentle transforming fingers
                of the Potter at the wheel.

Tonight we are invited to risk together.

To risk believing in an eternal transforming
        that is always at work
        but never captured.
To risk letting go of our own fragment
        and be foolish enough to jump out into the in-between,
        foolish enough to risk telling each other our little piece
                of the only word which connects us,
                        The Good News.
        The news that all division is overcome,
        all fragmentation breached
                in the body of Jesus
                        given over.

So let us enter into prayer together.

        Our transforming God, it is your action alone
                which holds us in being together.

Give us the courage
　　to reach out tonight
　　to embrace the whole of your creation in trust.
Give us eyes and ears and fingertips
　　to sense your transforming touch at work within us
　　and all about us.
Hold us in the cleft of the rock
and let us know the finest whisper of the breeze as you pass by.
Let us know ourselves as the living body of your Son, Jesus,
　　who is the Christ,
　　at work in your creation and giving you delight,
　　　　even now and forever. Amen.

BLESSING PRAYER

It is fitting, Lord, that we praise you.
　　At all times.
　　In season and out.

We praise you in a special way as we recall that
　　again and again down through our history
　　　　you have broken through the shells
　　　　　　of our disconnectedness
　　　　and called us forth into transformation.

You sent us men and women
　　to transform our imaginations
　　and our faulty understandings
　　　　of what you were about in our world.

You sent a shepherd to be a king,
　　and you sent Jeremiah to show us that
　　　　exile just might mean liberation.
You sent a pagan king to save your people
　　when all the official prophets missed the point.

You sent us Gandhi when we were lost in just-war theories,
     and Rosa Parks to tell us that her feet hurt.

You continue to invite us to find you in all the most unlikely places.

And so we join this whole interconnected universe
     which you have made your home,
          in praising you in the words of Isaiah:

          Holy, holy, holy Lord, God of power and might.
          Heaven and earth are full of your glory.
          Hosanna in the highest.
          Blessed is he who comes in the name of the Lord.
          Hosanna in the highest.

Above all we celebrate your definitive presence in our world,
     in Jesus the Christ.

He has taken on himself all the tones and colors of us all,
     the hues of your whole creation.
But by offering himself into death in obedience to you
     he has transformed every color.
He has become the answer of all creation
     to your invitation that we share in your work
          of renewing the earth —
               by being free to hand it over.

We recall how it was on that night
     when his own transformation was to be fulfilled.
He was with his friends —
     connected,
     and yet fully aware
          how fragile was their grasp,
          how weak their hold.

Then he drew on his deepest bond,
      his trust in your eternal faithfulness.
And he rose from table
    took some bread,
        blessed you,
           broke it,
              and gave it away.
He said,
    "Take this, all of you.
      Eat it. It is my body handed over for you and for all."

And when they had finished the meal he took the wine.

And he said,
    "Take and drink this.
      This cup is the new covenant in my blood.
      It is being poured out for you and for all
      so that creation might be transformed,
      from the emptiness of hunger
        to the fullness of life.
    You do these same things as you remember me."

Lord, we do remember.
    We remember his life among us.
    We remember his passage through transforming death.
    And above all we remember the day of his resurrection,
      that you have made him the Christ,
      the beginning of our resurrection.

So together with the praise he gives you even now,
    we pray together with the whole church
    joined with us around the earth,
      that you will continue your transforming work in us.

Make of us a people free to care and to act,
>   to make this earth the place of your dwelling
>   And your delight,
>   a world of peace and justice.

We pray together with Jesus,
>   for it is through him
>   and with him
>   and in him
>   that you are blessed and praised,
>   our transforming God,
>   in the Holy Spirit,
>   now and forever. Amen.

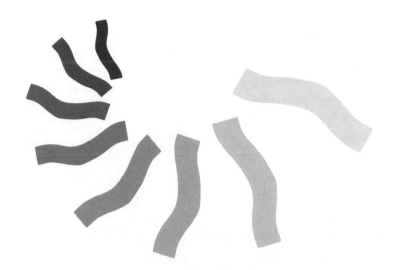

4. THE GOD WHO CONTINUES TO CREATE

GATHERING

Our loving Creator,
> you continually draw all of the elements of this creation
>> into the fullness of life,
>> to forms beyond our wildest imaginings.

This day,
> in the risen body of Jesus the Christ,
> you unfold for us what our creation,
> our body,
>> is meant to be.

In him we are set free
> from our unbelief,
>> into a world where we see one another
>>> as sister and brother;
> from our cynicism and despair,
>> into a world where hope becomes our birthright;
> from our isolation and self-pity,

into a world where the deeds
of caring,
justice,
and peace
really happen.
Out of the fullness of this creation in ourselves, we bless you.

We pray that your Easter Spirit may dwell within us
all our days
so that we may share in the incomparable privilege
of tending the garden of your creation
until it discloses forever the fullness of your infinite,
tender love.

We pray in the name of Jesus,
the first-born of the new creation,
through whom you are glorified
this day and always,
till time be no more. Amen.

COMMISSIONING

Before we enter upon our blessing-prayer, I invite you to accept a new commission: *(Participants respond each time: "I accept my commission.")*

In the name of Jesus Christ,
who is the first-born of many from the dead,
who has carried the elements of the old creation
once and for all
through the veil
and beyond the powers of death:
I call upon you and commission you
to reverence this earth
and work to develop all its tiniest potentialities;

I call upon you and commission you
>> to be builders and not destroyers,
>> conserving creators and not marauding consumers;
I call upon you and commission you
>> to proclaim hope for this world
>>> in the face of the nay-sayers;
>> to contemplate and search out its pregnant truth
>>> beneath the illusions of its sterility;
I call upon you and commission you
>> to give this world a chance to be;
>> to play and find your delight here,
>> and so to be at one with our God
>>> who finds joy
>>>> in sharing this earth with us.

BLESSING PRAYER

Indeed, it is right and just
>> that we give you thanks and praise
>>> at all times
>>> and in all places.
For there is no time,
> there is no place
> where you are not spinning the potter's wheel
> and sinking your hands into the moist clay of your creation,
>> shaping it
>>> again and again,
>>>> over and over and over,
>>>> to new forms for your delight.

You made the pristine cosmos unimaginably vast.

And then you chose a smaller place,
>> a place where you yourself could walk with us
>>> in the cooling evening.

And even when we turned our backs on the garden
and misused your creation
    to fashion false gods,
        you used the waters of the earth to cleanse us.
        You took up your station
        in the rainbow
            and the manna
            and the pillar of fire and cloud.
You let kings and pharaohs of this world
    scatter us
    and drive us
        like sheep —
        all the while preparing for us
            new lands,
            new waters,
            a new earth.
With all these creations that have gone before us,
    with all those people who kept your word alive
        and passed it on from one to another
            like a faint ember
            or a precious handful of water,
    we sing your praises
    as the prophet Isaiah taught us to say
        long centuries ago:

        Holy, holy, holy Lord, God of power and might.
        Heaven and earth are full of your glory.
        Hosanna in the highest.
        Blessed is he who comes in the name of the Lord.
        Hosanna in the highest.

Finally you shaped your perfect creation,
    the completion
        of earth
        and air

and fire
and water,
  Jesus
  who was to become the Christ,
  the fullness of the cosmos.

In a finite body,
amid finite people,
in a brief span of time,
  he showed us the highest wonder of creation:
    he gave it all,
    he gave himself,
      away.

It was the night that the people
  of his making
    were to reject him
    and drive him out of the city.
He joined his closest friends —
  and his known betrayer —
    in a meal.

And then he did a new thing.

He took the bread of the season;
he consecrated himself to you;
and he gave the bread to them, saying,
  "Take this,
    all of you;
    eat of it.
  This is my body handed over for you."
And then he took the cup
  of gladness
  and suffering,
and he said,

"This cup is the new covenant in my blood;
drink from it,
all of you,
    for it is being poured out
    so that you may have the fullness of life.
And when you do,
  remember me."

We do remember, creator God,
and in that remembering we are made whole together.

We are one
    with his life,
    his free passage into death,
    and the risen life you breathe
        into him
        and into us,
            his body.

We use that life
    and that breath
        to pray now.
We pray for all those who are joined with us in faith,
    that we may know you as he did:
        in the very doing
        of truth and peace and justice.

We do all these things in the name
    and the Spirit of Jesus.
For it is through him
    and with him
    and in him
        that all glory and honor are yours, Eternal Creator,
        In the unity of the Holy Spirit,
            now and forever. Amen.

5. AT HOME IN CREATION

We gather together
      to celebrate the central meal of all human history.

The meal at which our very God
      — gentle Father,
    ever-faithful Mother —
          joins us at the table
          and feeds us with eternal life
              in the person of Jesus of Nazareth.

But before we partake of that meal,
      before we commune,
          we must search out its beginnings.

In the stuff of creation.

The stuff out of which comes the bread and wine;
      the same stuff
          which is shaped into the body and blood of the Lord;

the same stuff of which is fashioned our body,
      destined to become his body in our time.

The body of this creation is very ancient.
    It is the womb of all good,
    and all evil.
      It is fascinating.
      And it is terrifying.
      Because it is the abode of the holy.

We must know this body
    in all its wondrous power
      as well as its miserable failure;
    its ambivalence and contradiction,
      as well as its revelation.

We must enter into its death potentiality
    if we would grasp its life reality.

Let us hear the voices of the elements of creation,
    the elements of his body and ours.

THE VOICE OF EARTH

I am earth.

Shape and contour
    and stability;
      the rock of the mountain
      and the loam of the delta.

I hold the seeds of life
    and I cradle your fuel.

Eternally my platelets inch their way upon the waters,
until their crushing force begets
mighty Alps and Andes.

I root your cedars
and your crocuses,
bed your roads,
and anchor your dams.

You are born of me,
you do not own me.

I can lash and whip you
and spew forth my power
in quakes
and volcanoes
and avalanches.

And still you violate me.

Instead of feeding, I am constrained to poison;
for I have become the repository of all your deadly waste.
You wrench my resources from me
and build the weapons of your own self-destruction.

But I am not overcome.

I serve One higher
and stronger
and wiser
and more caring
than you.

I have been the soil of your origin.
And I will be the place of your final transformation.

THE VOICE OF AIR

To find me you must cease your endless looking,
    and attune your sensitive hearing,
      your finest touch.
I am air.

I filled the sails when your ancestors set forth in search of new life.
    I drove the mills that ground their grain.

Without me no bird flies,
    no seed drifts to its new place of germination.

I am the warming breath of a mother on the face of her child,
    and the slender thread
        that holds someone among the living in C.P.R.

Without me the fire could do no harm.

Do not think you own me.

I will carry the lovely melodies of your songs,
    but I can also toss you like a rag doll
      when it suits me.
I can suck you up into my tornado
    and spit you out like broken toothpicks.

Your "secure" homes are like so many anthills
    before my hurricane blasts.

I course within you.
    You use me for your curses
      and your false promises
      and your idle boasting
      and posturing.

But one day you will breathe me forth one last time
      and I will continue on with my work
        as the servant of our common Master.

THE VOICE OF FIRE

Deep in your most primeval sensation I reside.

I am fire, the hearth by which you huddle
      against the icy darkness
        of endless night.

It is I who am at the source, the sun.

My rays beget the life-power that cracks the dry seed-pod;
I call the sprout forth
      until in an imperceptible heave
      it pushes the earth aside
        and stretches up to my warmth.

I sear your mill-ground flour
      and turn it into food;
I penetrate the bud
      and stretch the grape
        until it bursts with the juice of life itself.

And finally I become your energy,
      your passion,
      your desire:
        the possibility of your love.

Tread gently as you handle me.
I am capable of rage; I can be all-consuming.
      Loose me and nothing will stand in my way.

Misuse me and my name becomes
        Dachau
        and Auschwitz
        and Hiroshima.
My radiation can initiate love
        or cremation,
    a pulsing heart
        or a molten furnace.

I am in you. It is you who are the earth or the oven.

THE VOICE OF WATER

Your beginnings are in me,
    in the cushioned sloshing of your mother's womb.

I am the water
    out of which life slithered onto the beaches of the land.

For thousands of years,
    and to this day,
        I lap the shores
        and tumble over countless falls
            in breath-taking beauty.
I capture all the shades and hues
    as I glisten in the rainbow,
        and I quiver like a living pearl
            on the tip of a leaf.

The whole of the thirsting earth cranes its neck
    to capture a drop of my soothing rain.
I teem with life in all the seas of the earth.

Oh, but I am always at work,
       eating away at your secure coasts,
       wearing away your rich soil
       and even your rocks.

You seek to tame me —
       and I become the unbridled flood
       which sweeps away all in its course.
You foul me with your toxins
       and I become your grave.

And to think that I can be the seat of your Baptism.

It is out of this stuff
       and into this world of risk
              and ambiguity
              and contradiction
       that God hurls Jesus,
              bearing all its possibility
              and all its tragedy.

And it is in the same stuff that he chooses to live out his life
       in his continuing body, his people;
              in us.

Let us take some time to be in touch with the elements
       of this ambivalent world,
       pulling itself apart
              in the effort to save itself.

[If this is common prayer, the participants are invited to share personal experiences, stories of potentiality fulfilled or thwarted.]

And so we go to the meal of the Lord. We enter Jesus' room,
    where we will discover
            that the elements of creation can indeed be seduced
                into harmony,
                into the deeds of love and justice and peace —
            but where we will also learn
                at what great price that fulfillment is won.

Blessing Prayer

Lord, it is right that we praise you.
For you continue to labor over your creation.
Down through the ages you continue to re-fashion the elements
    in ever-new models suited to the needs of your people.

You shape Moses and Miriam;
        Esther and Rachel,
        David and Isaiah
        and all the *anawim.*

You even use the flood and the exile,
        the Pharoahs and Cyrus,
                to shape the consciousness of your people.

Gradually and lovingly you, the Potter, prepare the stuff of this world
        until it becomes the womb of a lowly Jewish girl,
                the place of your ultimate meeting with your creation
                    in the body of Jesus of Nazareth.

We bless you that he has pitched his tent in creation,
        in the stuff of our own bodies;
that you choose this malleable matter
        as the seed-bed of your final revelation of your care
                for this world.

We remember once more how,
    in his own body,
    he expressed who he was
        through the elements of our bodies.

He touched her and the fever left her (Matthew 8:14-15).

*"Why are you fearful?" And with that he rebuked the winds
and the sea. And all was calm again (Mark 4:39-40).*

He breathed on them (John 20:22).

*Jesus came from Galilee to the Jordan to be baptized by John.
John tried to dissuade him. But Jesus replied, "Leave it like this for
the time being; it is fitting that we should in this way do all that
righteousness demands (Matthew 3:13-15).*

*In the fourth watch of the night he came walking toward them
on the lake (Mark 6:48).*

*He took the man aside, away from the crowd, put his fingers
into his ears and touched his tongue with spittle (Mark 8:33).*

And we remember where it all led.

It was in Jerusalem,
    toward which he had set his face from the beginning.
He was at table with his friends
    — and with an enemy —
        celebrating the history of their people at a meal.

And then he did a new thing
    with the elements that lay before him,
    ordinary fruit of the earth.
He raised them up and said,

"This is my body,
and this is my blood.
My body will be given over
and my blood poured out,
as a new,
and everlasting,
covenant with you.
Take them;
eat and drink together;
and as you do,
remember me."

And so we stand,
loving and faithful God,
at the center of all creation.

We will eat the body and drink the blood of him
who is the center of all creation.

We will eat the body and drink the blood of him
who is the fulfillment
of all that creation can become,
the embodiment
of love
and justice
and peace.

In the power of his willing entry into death
and Your gift of the Spirit
in his risen life,
we pray that that same transforming Spirit
may enliven us,
your people
and his body.

We do not ask to be removed
      from all conflict
      and contradiction,
            because we know that our salvation will be found
            only in the opaque world
                  where his flesh touches ours.

We pray rather that
      through this life-giving food and drink
      we may do the deeds
            of truth
            and peace
            and justice
      which are the sign that he lives now
      and transforms your creation
            for the fulfillment of your loving plan.

Bring us,
      through all our deaths,
            to the life he shares with you.

For it is through him
      and with him
      and in him
            that you are blessed and praised,
            our loving God,
                  in the Spirit,
                        now and forever. Amen.

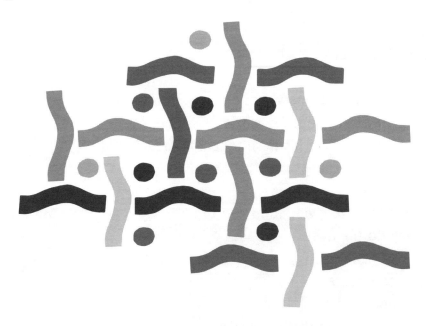

6. The Web of Life

Greeting

We gather as many individuals who come from many different places
and bring many different experiences and many different histories.
We have internalized many different voices during our lives
and we carry an enormous number of characters within our internal,
"inside-us" communities.

Sometimes we seem to be a whole Babel all by ourselves.
And as if that were not enough, we even hold within us
many different countries, and cultures, and bits of earth;
asphalt and frangipani, teakwood and sycamore and dioxin.
Let's pause for a moment and each gather up our personal worlds.
Hold them in the palms of your hands and bring them
into our celebration.

In our prayer we want to see those worlds from a new perspective —
from the eyes of our God.

Some would say that our separate worlds are only illusion;
that all is simply one without distinction.

John Donne said that no one is an island.

Someone else said recently that what John Donne should have said is
that *everyone* is an island, but that islands aren't what they seem to be.
Islands are all really islands, but they are also connected.

Our God, the one god of the one creation, invites us to see reality
as one seamless web of life. The web is really made of many
weavings and many colors. Each has its own place (as hard as it
may be for us to find that place) and each touches directly only a
limited number of other pieces. Some of the threads were woven
in long ago and have affected the direction of all that followed after
them — and yet any single new piece carries the power to change
the whole meaning of all that preceded it. Bright and splashy,
obscure and drab — none finally has meaning except within the
ultimate pattern. Some parts of the web we can see very clearly but
often the part that carries it all is least in evidence. Even the gaps
and the holes — and the mistakes — all "belong." The web might
satisfy some Promethean illusion of ours if the holes and mistakes
and sin were not there, but utopias have no "where"; they are not
the reflection of our very real God.

In our prayers a very familiar — but very strange — figure will be
showing up and making us take different positions within the web,
guiding us to see it ever more fully. Jesus.

> Someone from a little hill town in the Middle East?
> Just another one of the pieces, however commanding?
> Its beginning and end, the center of the cosmos?
> A monstrous rip in the pattern?
>   — or the very key to the pattern,
>   the pattern incarnate?

Let us try
      to listen to him,
      to watch,
      to be inside his skin
            as he lives the pattern.

Three things our God tells us:
      that we also create the pattern,
      that the weaving is what our universe is all about,
      and that the web is the object of God's infinite delight.

And as we move now towards our symbolic web,
      I invite you to carry your scraps and patches
            in the palms of your hands.
Bring them to the table
      and share them with your table companions.
Ask one another:
      where do you see the pattern?
      Where are the unseen connections?

Bring your piece and share it with us:
      people,
      events,
      insights,
      objects,
      bits of Scripture,
      bits of yourself
            — for you are in the web with us.

(Procession to the worship space, where a large network of fabric stringers, much like a spider's web, is spread out. Some of it may already be woven with fabric scraps, to which the participants will add further pieces as they integrate their own experiences into the total web.)

PRAYER

God our Creator,
Father and Mother,
      you are the eternal weaver,
      we are but pieces in your seamless web.
And yet you have also invited us to weave it with you,
      to share in the pattern which is Jesus.

Through the Eucharist we share this night
      teach us to see ourselves
      and the web of our life
          as you see it;
              feed us
              and nourish us
              and empower us

          to build the bits and pieces
              of our lives
              and of our world
          into the web that will give you delight:
              a world of care,
              a world where pain is touched with compassion
                  and joy is embraced with hunger.

Immerse us into the life of Jesus the Christ,
      who unveils and discloses you
      and makes you very near to us,
      who is your glory
          now and for ever. Amen.

Prayer over the Gifts

The web of meaning,
the food and drink of life —-
    all are the same reality.
You share it with us,
    our provider God.
And now transform it.

Transform *us*
    so that we can see it for what it is,
    the body and blood of Jesus
        given
    so that all the pieces might have meaning,
        might be known as one:
    your life lived out in your creation forever and ever. Amen.

Blessing Prayer

Our creator God,
the center of the web of our life,
    it is right,
    it is our privilege
        to thank you and bless you at all times,
            in all seasons.
On this night we seek to remember.

To remember the whole web,
    to remember our place within it.

We remember that we are sprung from the earth,
    that no matter how high we soar
        it is your wondrous earth that supports us —
        and we bless you.

We bless you for each blade of grass
>   and each solid rock,
>   for the rivers
>   and the deserts
>   and the jungles.

We remember that we are in a giant web of people
>   stretching back to the beginning of known time
>   and around our whole globe.

We remember that we belong to the searchers and seers
>   who have sought out the pattern
>   even as they created it,
>   again and again
>   in every human hour.

We rejoice at the mystery of our oneness
>   with men and women of so many different times and cultures,
>   with a David and a Ruth,
>   with a Magdalene and a Zachaeus and a Gamaliel
>   and an unknown widow
>   who gave her only two cents.

We are one with a Catherine of Siena
>   and a John XXIII,
>   a Michelangelo
>   and a Picasso
>   and an Ingmar Bergman,
with a bag lady
>   and a Dalai Lama —
>   and we bless you.

The web is one,
>   and the web is yours,
>   and the web is holy.

And so in union with the whole of the web,
      your creation,
      we sing:

      Holy, holy, holy Lord, God of power and might.
      Heaven and earth are full of your glory.
      Hosanna in the highest.
      Blessed is he who comes in the name of the Lord.
      Hosanna in the highest.

The web is one.

But you have given it
      a center.
A center totally like us,
      one in whom we can recognize the privilege that is ours
            in the call to continue the design
                  and the weaving,
            and to know the price
                  that the weaving will exact from us.

We bless you for Jesus,
      who takes his life from this earth
      and hands it back to the earth
            in the fullest freedom
            because he knows
                  the mystery.

He knows that
      you are the faithful One,
            and because he knows,
                  he fulfills the pattern himself
                      to the fullest.

And so we remember this night
    that he has empowered us
    to fulfill his own mission
        when
        on the eve of his own most unjust death
        he gathered us around him.
He took the bread
    of this earth
and the cup
    of its wine;
        he blessed you
        and he fed us
    as he said,
        "Take this.
        Eat it.
        It is my body.
        And drink this cup.
        It is my blood.
            It is being given
            and poured out
                for you
        so that your life may be restored
        and you may find your place
            in the pattern of my Father's creation.

When you do these things,
    remember me."

And so, our faithful God,
    we remember
    and we are re-membered
        with all those who share this Eucharist with us
            around this earth.

Enlighten us through this food and drink;
    teach us the way,
        the pattern;
    empower us with the Spirit of Jesus
        so that we may love
            as he loved,
        heal
            as he healed,
        hunger and thirst for justice
            as he hungered and thirsted.

Weave us ever more deeply
    into your mystery,
    your plan,
        so that we may be your delight.

We make our prayer with Jesus
    and in him and through him,
        for he gives you glory
            now and forever. Amen.

7. EASTER AND THE WEB OF LIFE

A BLESSING OF WATER

God of all the elements,
    you have made the web of your creation
        depend on the waters of our earth.
Without the snows and rains
    our land cracks open,
      the beauty of our shrubs and trees and flowers
        becomes a mere memory,
    and we shrivel up
        and die.

It was with the waters of the flood
    that you cleaned your earth —
but on the same waters
    you saved your people.
You made the waters of the sea part
    to open the way to our freedom
and with the same waters
    you destroyed those who would make us slaves.

Your pattern,
     Jesus,
entered the waters
     in humble acceptance
          of his oneness with a sinful people —
and also transformed the water
     of everyday human joy
          into the wine
              of a heavenly banquet.

Bless this water this day,
     compassionate God.

As its drops touch us,
     teach us
          that the blood that courses in our veins
              is one with all the peoples of our earth,
          that it is one with the blood of Jesus.

Teach us
     not to despise our own flesh
          but to love our real selves,
     the body of your whole creation,
          which,
              because it is one with Jesus,
              delights you
                 now and forever. Amen.

A Re-Commitment Rite for Easter

During these days we have tried to insert ourselves more deeply
into the web of life, to weave ourselves and the pieces of our lives
into the common, humble, lovely fabric of God's creation. And so
I ask you now:

Is it your intention now to continue to search out ever more fully the pattern of our loving God in all your experiences, to resist the voices that whisper only meaninglessness and despair?

Is it your intention now to follow the pattern, Jesus, as he takes on the whole mystery of life through death, and refuse to be overcome by our own sin and failure but cling to the God who weaves beauty out of dry thatch?

Is it your intention not to cut yourself off from the web of God's people but rather to contribute your gifts, your pains, and your joys to the enriching of your sisters' and brothers' lives?

(Sprinkling with blessed water:) Then may the holy God of all creation touch you with the waters of life so that your very being may exemplify the pattern established in Jesus the Christ, the beginning and the end, the center of all being, now and forever. Amen.

Blessing Prayer

God,
>the seamless robe
>>of your life
>>and your creation
>appears to us at times
>>to be rent
>>and ripped.

But you are constant in your weaving.
>For your steadfast love and mercy we bless you.

We bless you
>that the exile and slavery of our people
>>was the place where you taught them
>>their need to be rooted in you.

It is there that you taught them hope.

And it was in their liberation
      that you taught us the fulfillment of your promise.

Again and again
      out of our sin
          and death
      you have fashioned resurrection
          and new life.

And so we join the whole of your creation
      in blessing you as we sing:
          Holy, holy, holy Lord, God of power and might.
          Heaven and earth are full of your glory.
          Hosanna in the highest.
          Blessed is he who comes in the name of the Lord.
          Hosanna in the highest.

Above all, our God,
      we thank you for the resurrection of Jesus,
      the beginning of our own new life.

We thank you
      that the message of his rising
          is that the web is not broken.
The risen Christ who shared bread and fish
      with his friends by the side of the lake
          is the same Jesus
          who asked the woman at the well for a drink of water.

The hands he offers us
      bear the holes
      where real nails ripped his flesh —
          but in the power of the resurrection they are transformed
          so that even we who have not seen may believe
              in the wholeness of the web.

In seamless continuity with his own action
      and in the power of his risen life
      we now do what he commanded us to do:
            we remember,
            we touch the deepest core of our lives —
            and we are made whole.

That night he took bread into his hands
      and so we take bread into our hands.

We bless you as he did,
and we repeat his words:
      "This is my body.
            Take it
            and eat it,
                  for it is for you that it is broken
                  and given."

We take the cup
      as he took the cup,
and blessing you we say
      what he said:
            "Drink this,
                all of you.
            It is the cup of my blood.
            With it I establish a covenant
                that will never be broken,
            so that sin may no longer have power
                But my Spirit may empower you to live
                    as I do.
            Do these things in memory of me."

We are one with you,
      our God,
            in the Spirit of Jesus.

In the power of that Spirit we pray
       that your life may become ever more manifest in us,
           your people.
And especially in that portion of your people he has claimed
       as his gathering,
       his church.
We pray for our brother, the pope,
       that he may lead us with wisdom;
for our brothers and bishops,
       that they may be deeply rooted in
           and responsive to
       the cares and hopes of their churches;
for all those involved in service
       in the name of your Son,
           that they may recognize him in the least of his little ones;
and finally for all your people,
       that they may do his works
       and fulfill the pattern
           simply by caring for their brothers and sisters.
Empower us
       with the memory
       and the deeds of love
           performed by all the friends who have gone before us,
           with whom we hope to share
               and enjoy the contemplation of your wisdom
       when we meet again.

We make this prayer in the name
       and in the power of Jesus,
           for it is through him
               and with him
               and in him
       that you are blessed and praised now and forever. Amen.

8. SANCTUARY

Tonight we gather in sanctuary for a brief time. The sanctuary of our domestic church. It may sound pretentious to call us a "church", because as a total body our interaction is transient; some of us meet only at these times of prayer together.

But then again, maybe that will be characteristic of church for our time: much less settled-down communities, but rather people who gather together from time to time around the Good News of Jesus, are nourished with his life and feed each other, and then free each other to go forth and be about very different pieces of the work of the kingdom.

Sanctuary. The dictionary says: "a holy place, a place set aside for worship; a place of refuge or protection, where fugitives are immune from arrest." We hear it and we see images. Refugees; illegal aliens; people who are 'undocumented'; people wading across the Rio Grande, with other people on their backs; church people, Jesus people, driving out into the night to places of rendezvous, bringing strangers to their churches and homes; men and women with masks to hide their identities, standing before microphones and telling their stories; men and women standing in court to hear their sentences.

We experience the mystery of evil and pain, but also the excitement of courage and holiness. We are torn, because we participate in both realities. We are implicated in the system that creates the injustice, and we are one body with those who resist its effects; they are our sisters and brothers.

The danger is that we will make sanctuary something "out there." something we watch. When, in reality, it is we who are refugees, aliens in a strange land, always in need of sanctuary and shelter.

We are citizens, to be sure. Citizens of the U.S.A. or Canada or Uganda, or *(mention states, cities, towns, suburbs appropriate for your community)*. We are each members of many different layers of community. But way down inside ourselves we are aware that these are only the arenas in which we enact a different citizenship, a deeper identity. We sense that we are God's people. In Jesus we have been touched, and that touch has stirred energies in us that put us in pilgrimage. Martin Luther King reminds us that we are called to be creatively maladjusted in this world. We are always looking for those who have been touched in the same way we have been touched, who have heard the same story and entered the same mystery, who hunger and thirst after the same food and drink, because we are drawn by the same vision and dream.

And so we gather. We find a place together; we *make* a place together and it becomes especially holy. We acknowledge our difference together and we become sanctuary for each other — protection and refuge, a shelter to warm the dream; a place where it's alright to be alien.

Let's stop for a moment and think of all the communities in which we find and offer sanctuary, the places where we discover the pain of our alienation and the mysterious gift of companionship.

("Passports" are distributed; time for quiet reflection.)

Now let us proceed to the inner sanctuary of our common table, where we will share the story and the journey of the one who is most different and most one with us, Jesus of Nazareth, as he is cast outside the city and thereby makes the whole cosmos his home and ours forever.

Readings

(Readers are scattered about the worship space and proclaim various texts with pauses in-between.)

□ She wrapped him round, and laid him in a manger, because there was no room for them at the inn *(Luke 2:7)*.

□ Herod intended to search for the child and do away with him. So Joseph got up and, taking the child and his mother with him, left that night for Egypt, where he stayed until Herod was dead. And a voice was heard in Ramah, sobbing and loudly lamenting; it was Rachel weeping for her children, refusing to be comforted because they were no more *(Matthew 2:13-17)*.

□ What description can I find for this generation? It is like children shouting to each other as they sit in the market place: We played the pipes for you, and you wouldn't dance; we sang dirges, and you wouldn't be mourners. For John came, neither eating nor drinking, and they say, "He is possessed." The Son of Man came, eating and drinking, and they say, "Look, a glutton and a drunkard, a friend of tax collectors and sinners." *(Matthew 11:16-19)*

□ He came to Nazareth, where he had been brought up, and they handed him the scroll of the prophet Isaiah. And he said, "This text is being fulfilled today even as you listen." And they were astonished and said, "Where did the man get this wisdom? This is the carpenter's son, surely?" And they would not accept him. Jesus said to them, "A prophet is only despised in his own country and in his own house." They were enraged, sprang to their feet and hustled him out of the town; and they took him up to the brow of the hill their town was built on, intending to throw him down the cliff *(Luke 4:16-29)*.

□ He met Philip and said, "Follow me." Philip found Nathaniel and said to him, "We have found the one Moses wrote about in the Law." Nathaniel said, "Can anything good come out of Nazareth?" *(John 1:43-46)*

BLESSING PRAYER

Our creator God, we bless you.

We have heard our story
        in the story of Jesus.
That story has fed us
        and challenged us
                again and again
                        as a people
                                across the centuries;
                        and as individuals,
                                at so many turns along our journey of life.
It brings us to this holy moment
        when together we enter into his deepest estrangement,
        the moment
                when you transform his body
                        into our eternal sanctuary
                and empower us
                        to be his transforming presence
                                in your wondrous universe.

He gathered with his community
        to eat and drink the meal of their people's story.
He sang their songs and psalms.

He said, I call you not servants but friends."
And he said, "One of you will betray me this night."
And saying "Where I an going you cannot come now,"
  he rose from table
  and did a new thing.

He took the bread that lay before them
  and he said to the one he called Father,
   "They are strangers in the world,
    as I am.
   Consecrate them by the truth.
   You have sent me into the world;
   I have sent them into the world,
    and for their sake I consecrate myself
    that they too may be consecrated."
He broke the bread
  and gave it to them, with the words
   "Take this. Eat it. It is my body,
    broken and given for you."
And so with the cup.
   "Take and drink from this cup.
    It is my blood poured out,
     for you and for all,
     an irrevocable commitment.
Do these same things when you gather in memory of me."

We are gathered. We do remember.
  And so with Isaiah we sing the mystery of God's holy presence:

   Holy, holy, holy Lord, God of power and might.
   Heaven and earth are full of your glory.
   Hosanna in the highest.
   Blessed is he who comes in the name of the Lord.
   Hosanna in the highest.

In this memory we are empowered by you our God
    to become sanctuary,
    to receive sanctuary.
And so we take into our hearts
    all those who are joined with us in a special way this night;
    those with whom we share
        the journey and the story,
        the estrangement and the solidarity,
        the sin and the grace,
        the death and the life. *(Pause.)*
We pray that we may be opened
    to the power you will give us:
    the power
        to receive with compassion
        and to hand ourselves over in our brokenness;
    the power
        to find in our many earthly citizenships
        the arenas for transformation of your cosmos
            into a place of justice and peace and love,
            a place for your delight.
We pray with him who continues
    to fashion us into his own body,
    Jesus of Nazareth
        who has become the Christ of the universe.
    Through him
    and with him
    and in him
        you are blessed
        and praised
            in the unity of the Spirit,
            our creator God, forever and ever. Amen.

9. COMMUNITY — OUR SANCTUARY

GREETING

Welcome again to our sanctuary.

Who are we? We search all the signs of the cosmos and our
history for the meaning of life. We walk with Jesus through exile to
exultation. We are an Easter people. Our story is the Easter story,
the story of creation made whole — and holy.

We have been admitted into the mystery, the plan hidden since the
beginning of time. The whole cosmos is the abode of the holy, meant
to be sanctuary for all, a dwelling place for our God and the people
of our God. The mystery begun in the first burst of energy at the
beginning of creation continues in every particle of our bodies, in the
body of the Christ.

We are citizens, not just of our local community or our city or our
state or even of our nation. We are citizens of our planet. On this
day of the new creation, new beginning, I invite you now to take upon

yourself the responsibilities of planetary citizenship as a follower of the one who by loving this world to the extreme of his own death, has become the Christ of the universe. *("Planetary passports" can be distributed and a pledge of commitment recited, with song.)*

And so we take our places by the tomb of Jesus, not knowing quite what else to do. And the word of the ever-faithful God comes to us in the loving act of caring women who come to anoint a body.

Luke 23:55-24:11 is read.

The story appeared to them to be nonsense, as so often it appears to men and women of our age, and to us. We puzzle, and search God's word still more. And Paul unfolds for us the full meaning of the transformation of Jesus of Nazareth into the Christ of the whole cosmos.

Colossians 1:13-27 is read.

BLESSING PRAYER

Lord, rightly do we praise you,
>   for that is the only way we can be
>   what you have made us to be.

There is only one food
and only one drink,
>   one loaf
>   and one vessel.

The whole of our transformation is enacted
>   and centered
>   in the transformation of one human,
>   In Jesus.

Jesus of Nazareth
        and Jerusalem
        and Golgotha,
Jesus of Corinth
        and Ephesus
        and Rome,
Jesus of Geneva
        and Washington
        and Warsaw
        and Sarajevo.

He lived,
        and he has chosen to continue to live,
                in us.
He made friends
and loved enemies,
        and he does these things in us,
                his people.
He died
        and he continues to share
                our deaths.

He has been transformed
        from a dead body to a life-giving presence,
                breathing
                and touching
                and in-spiriting,
        and by his touch
        and his breath
                he has taken on our fragile shell
                as his continuing body,
                        turning our blindness into vision,
                        our feebleness into strength,
                        our timidity into courage,
                        our violence into the deeds of peace.

But that was not enough.

He centered his own act of life-producing death
in the meal he celebrated
and continues to celebrate
          with us.

There is only one eating
and only one drinking.
          In this act
                    we are connected with the whole of creation,
          with all that was
                    or is
                    or ever shall be.

You know how it was.
          He was celebrating his final meal
                    with those he loved.
          He was going forward,
                    freely,
                              Into his own death,
                                        his own transformation.

And he suddenly arose from table
                    and did a new thing.
          He took the loaf,
          offered himself into his Father's hands,
                    and breaking the bread he said,
                              "Take this, each of you.
                                        Eat it.
                              It is my body-being-given,
                              my life being freely poured out.
                                        For you
                                        and for all."

And then the cup.

He said,
"Drink of this cup.
It is my blood.
A new covenant,
which encompasses
and enlivens
all other human covenants.
I am pouring it out freely.
Sin is being overcome.
Now,
and definitively.
The transformation will be accomplished.

You go and do these same things yourselves,
remembering me."

We do remember, Lord.

And we are re-membered.
We are made whole in your own transformation.
We are connected
as your one people
journeying down the ages.
And so we unite ourselves silently in adoration
with those who have passed on ahead of us —
with those who are being transformed with us
now
around our earth —
and even with those
to whom we will one day hand over this creation,
those still to be born
into the transforming process.

We do this, our God —
>Mother,
>Father —
>>together with him
>>who is the Alpha
>>and the Omega,
>>>Jesus your anointed Christ,
>>>for in him you are worshiped
>>>>and delighted
>>>>>now and forever. Amen.

(Bread and wine are shared.)

CONCLUDING PRAYER

Lord, we are made whole in these moments of communion.
But the illusions of our fragmentation
>and aloneness
>>hover always about our spirits.
May the food and drink we have shared
>continue to quicken us,
>>so that we may continue to reach out
>>>in the faith that you are there,
>>>in our sisters and brothers,
>>>and in our earth,
>>transforming us into your new creation.

May we continue to delight you
>as you see in us
>>the body and person of Jesus Christ
>>>glorifying you forever and ever. Amen.

10. A BONDED CREATION

GREETING

World spirit bonding. There is a mystery at work in our universe.
And in that smaller universe which is each one of us. We are invited,
not to put aside all the cares and confusions and pains of our many
worlds, to pretend they don't exist, but rather to bring them with us
to a deeper place inside us.

A place where we can let them be touched and illuminated by that
continuing mystery. A place where we can find a new perspective that
integrates them and lets us see the infinite significance of the smallest
piece of it all.

Perhaps most importantly, a place where we can be transformed by the
power of the Spirit into agents who share in the bonding energy,
into people whose spirits are ever attuned to that unifying urge even in
the darkest crannies of our apparent fragmentation and isolation and
brokenness, into people who in fact and in deeds do heal and unify
and bond this world together.

The old Gospel song — culturally conditioned, to be sure; but that's the way it always is with us humans — tells us "he's got the whole world in his hands." And it's profoundly true: creation, all of it, is cradled within the touch of our invisible God.

Profoundly true, but only half the truth. For the way of our creator God is to place that world in our hands as well. And so we can just as truthfully sing: "We've got the whole world in our hands." Not as masters, surely not as tamers of a hostile jungle. But as partners with Jesus, the one with whom we are to enflesh the transforming power of the creator of it all and thus bring infinite delight to our God.

And so you are invited now to take the whole world into your hands. Close your eyes gently. Then cup your hands lightly to receive and hold our world with care.

As you receive it, imagine its peoples — those you know and those you only imagine. Turn it around slowly and go to all the places you have known: the cities and seas and mountains and deserts and jungles and farms. Visit its barrios and its ghettos, go to its prisons and its favelas, tour its hi-tech labs and its missile silos. Circle that world and try to discover the deepest bondings that hold it together in spite of all its fissures and ruptures and apparently unbridgeable chasms.

Call up the spirits of those with whom you feel yourself particularly bonded — tied together with a web as delicate as gossamer or as sturdy as a cable that even death can't sever. Keep your eyes closed and don't be surprised at the way that world can become present to you.

(Quiet reflection and song while someone circles among the group and places a small world-globe in the cupped hands of each person.)

Mystery of mysteries! The bonding spirit has gifted each of us with a tiny world. Observe it
     and cherish it
     and wonder at it.

Its only distinctions are those given it by its creator:
>water and land,
>oceans and continents.

All the other boundaries are of our own making:
>nations and states and counties, cities and villages,
>townships and wards and precincts —
>>all arbitrary demarcations
>>and gerrymanderings:
>>>illusions to shield us from the challenge
>>>of otherness.

Seductive havens of false securities
which deprive us of the possibility
>of stretching to our full statures
>and growing to wholeness.

It is within us to become conscious bearers and reflectors of this whole glorious creation. In our time of special journeying with Jesus we will come to know more fully both the cost and the promise.

>We will see how large our hearts must become
>>if we are to embrace the whole of this world;
>we will come to know the strength of the forces
>>which fight against us
>>and draw us to settle for less;
>and on Easter we will be given the power
>>to stretch a bit farther out into the world
>>>we have yet to explore
>>and to find there the God who has been at work in us
>>>from the beginning.

We move now to the place of our eucharist and communion;
>take your world and its peoples with you in prayer.

(A large symbolic collage expressing a many-colored world is spread across the wall.)

Take some of the symbolic forms *(triangles, circles, free forms)*
provided there, and in silence place them on that world. Let them
stand for people you know who have called you beyond yourself
> into mystery
> and beauty
> and courage
> and search
> and integrity.

Then after we are all seated, perhaps you may want to tell us all who
they are and what is the bond for you — or perhaps you may simply
want to hold them in the richest space within your own spirit.

(Personal sharing time.)

READING: *The Cosmic Christ, in Ephesians and Colossians.*

☐ Now in Christ Jesus, you that used to be so far apart from us have
been brought very close, by the blood of Christ. For Christ is the
peace between us and has made the two into one and broken down
the barrier that used to keep them apart *(Ephesians 2:11-14)*.

☐ You are no longer aliens or foreign visitors; you are citizens like all
the saints, and part of God's household. . . . You are being built into a
house where God lives, in the Spirit *(Ephesians 2:19,22)*.

☐ God has let us know the mystery, the hidden plan so kindly made
in Christ from the beginning, to act upon when the times had run
their course to the end, that everything would be brought together
under Christ as head, everything in heaven and everything on earth
(Ephesians 1:9-10).

☐ In his own person Jesus killed hostility. Later he came to bring the
good news of peace, peace to you who were far away and peace to
those who were near at hand *(Ephesians 2:15-17)*.

☐ Christ is the image of the unseen God and the first-born of all creation, for in Christ were created all things in heaven and on earth, everything visible and everything invisible *(Colossians 1:15-16)*.

☐ You have put on a new self which will progress towards true knowledge the more it is renewed in the image of its creator; and in that image there is no room for distinction between Greek and Jew, between the circumcised and the uncircumcised, or between barbarian and Scythian, slave and free person. There is only Christ: everything and in everything *(Colossians 3:9-11)*.

PRESENTATION OF GIFTS

God of our holy world, you have called us to be conscious bearers of the mystery of your love for the work of your hands. Together with Jesus we lay that work before you in adoration and benediction. We ask you to bless this world which is his body and ours. We ask you to graft us ever more deeply within it, to make us ever more aware of the bond which makes us one single people of unvarying dignity, your creative love. All glory to you in the one Holy Spirit this night and all nights till night is no more. Amen.

BLESSING PRAYER

How right indeed
    that we should give you thanks and praise.
For you were not content
    to create us
    and to call us to share in your creating.

All along the way you have provided us
    with women and men
    like us
    in every land and culture,

who refused to let us settle for our illusions
but called us beyond ourselves
        to the vision of who we are
        and who we are to be.

You gave us Abraham and Sarah,
and you gave us Barbara Jordan and Nelson Mandela.

You bind us to Esther and Ruth and Mary,
and the cord can reach to a Filipino cardinal
        and thousands of nameless people
                who are willing to sit down before tanks
                and invite their brothers to lay down their military toys.

You tie us to men and women
        who sit for years on Death Row,
and to those who must shoulder the awesome responsibility
        for deciding to end a human life.

You challenge and support us
        across continents
        and across centuries.

We join the whole of this glorious cloud of witnesses in praising you
as we sing:

Holy, holy, holy Lord, God of power and might.
Heaven and earth are full of your glory.
Hosanna in the highest.
Blessed is he who comes in the name of the Lord.
Hosanna in the highest.

Above all, our creator God,
we praise you for this Jesus
        who summed up in his body the full glory of your creation.

He touched people
    and they were healed;
he was himself touched
    by the hands
    and the hair
      of a woman,
        and he was restored.

He made ordinary men and women cast out the demons
    of fear
    and ignorance,
      and he himself received a betrayer's kiss.

And by handing himself over freely into the mystery of death
    he has become the Christ,
    the first-born of the whole cosmos.
And then on a night
    so like this
    and so unlike any other,
      he expressed his last will
      and showed his fullest power,
        by giving his life away.

We recall the ancient story:

While they were at supper
    he acknowledged his betrayer
    and then he rose
    and did a new thing.

He took bread from the table before them. He broke it.
He said, "This is my body. Take it. And eat it."

And then he took a cup of wine.
He said, "This cup is the new covenant in my blood.

It is being poured out for the whole of this creation
so that the barriers which divide
        Jew and Greek,
        woman and man,
        slave and free —
so that all barriers may be removed
and this world may become
        what it is destined to be,
        my one single body.
Drink this cup and keep me ever fresh in your memory."

And so we do recall,
        source of all our life and being.
In the power of his Spirit
        we ask you to watch over the whole of your creation,
        to keep us conscious of our bond with all people everywhere.
        Join us with John Paul
            and Desmond Tutu,
        with Coretta King
            and Olaf Palme.
Join our spirit especially with all those who
        in quiet and unpretentious ways
            succeed in the miracle of loving their enemies.

We join our prayer with those of all the people
        who have gone before us through death
        and await us at the banquet table of your kingdom.
We make this prayer in the name
        and in the power of Jesus.
            Through him and with him and in him
                you are blessed and praised
                    with your holy Spirit,
                        now and forever. Amen.

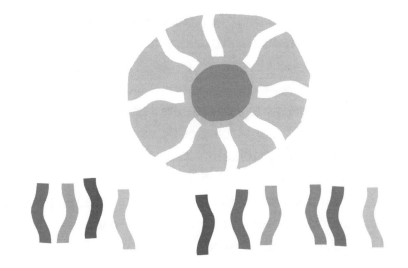

11. Easter: The Christ of the Cosmos

Greeting

When we gather for eucharist, we symbolically receive the whole world into our hands. We contemplate it with love and wonder. We join ourselves with its rich diversity of peoples and we try to search out the deepest invisible bonds that hold it together. We pray to enter more deeply into the mystery of the Christ, Jesus of Nazareth hurtled through the dark doorway of death and become the first-born of the whole cosmos, who draws all things — all of us — into wholeness and unity.

Today we hold him up once more before our God. As on every Easter, God gives the Christ back to us in the form of all the sources of new life which continually break through the tombs of our conformity and numbed consciousness and institutionalized blindness. The Christ returns to us as surprise; as the child of the aged and sterile Sarah in all of us; as the thunderous roar of a million dry bones with mouths that can cry out for justice; as rock musicians who can offer "live aid" to victims of African famine, and as the heart of a dead 14-year-old boy which beats on in the body of his girlfriend.

And so this morning as we prepare to receive the Good News of the most unexpected, we are invited to re-commit ourselves to the search for our hide-and-seek God.

☐ Do we commit ourselves to faith: to the unending work of letting go of the illusory crutch of sure ideologies by which we merely destroy our adversaries and build nothing?

☐ Do we commit ourselves to hope: to the stance that will not be denied, to an unflinching expectation that in the midst of death and failure and sin our God will continue to create new life?

☐ Do we commit ourselves to love: to becoming so eccentric as to find our center in the good of our neighbor — and even (miracle of miracles) the neighbor clothed in the garment of an enemy?

☐ And finally can we commit ourselves to adoration: to let God be God and Christ be our only messiah?

Then we are invited as a renewed and risen people to process toward the table of our communion with our God and one another.

PRAYER OVER THE GIFTS

Lord, we lay before you the gifts of your creation. They are the fruit of this precious earth. Men and women have harvested and crushed the grain and the grape; they have kneaded and baked the loaf, and fermented the juice, and they return to us now as food and drink. Just so was Jesus' word handed down and transformed to become our life. We ask you this day to transform our offering into the food and drink of eternal life, and so to transform us into bearers of that life to all we meet on our journey, wherever we go on this earth. We pray this in Jesus' name. Amen.

Blessing Prayer

It is so right and so fitting.
Above all on this day,
>> when you surprise us
>>> with life born out of death.
Down through the ages
>> you have continually challenged our expectations of this earth.

We were in exile in Egypt,
slaves without hope,
>> and you transformed our slavery into freedom.

We built you a temple
>> and you tore it down
>> and told us we were to be your living temple.

We tried to capture your life
>> in law chiseled on stone,
and you inscribed it instead
>> in the frail flesh of our fallible,
>>> human hearts.

We sought you in success
>> and security
>> and triumph,
and you have come to us again and again
>> in uprooting
>> and fragility
>> and ambiguity.

And so we join our hands and hearts
>> with the whole of this wondrous creation of yours.
We sing with the awe of the prophet
>> whose tongue was seared with a burning coal:

Holy, holy, holy Lord, God of power and might.
Heaven and earth are full of your glory.
Hosanna in the highest.
Blessed is he who comes in the name of the Lord.
Hosanna in the highest.

Above all
we are one this day with Jesus,
        your confirming
        and challenging
                word.

He broke through the barriers of his time.
        He sat by a well
                and talked
                        intimately
                                with a Samaritan
                                        woman
        and shocked his own disciples.

He made himself one
        with a leper
                by a touch,
and he told
        prostitutes
                they would enter his kingdom
                        before the righteous.

He dined
        with tax collectors
and told us
        we must become as receptive
                as little children.

And he showed us that death is not the final word.

We do now
> what he commanded us to do.

We tell the story
> and in the telling
>> his risen life is given to us.

They were at table,
he and his friends.
> They had sung the songs of his people.
> And they had tasted the bitter herbs.
> And then he took the bread that lay before them,
>> and the cup of wine.

He gave you thanks
and he said,
> "Take this
> and eat it.
>> It is my body
>> being handed over
>>> for you."

And "Drink of this cup.
> It is a new
>> and eternal
> covenant
>> in my blood,
>>> poured out so that my life may be in you
>>> and you in me.

Every time you celebrate in this way, remember me."

God of all the living,
> we remember him
> and we ponder
> and we adore.

He really died
but he really lives.

And through him
>   you have poured out your own breath
>   >   into us
>   >   and our whole world.

It is your breath which bonds us with this world.
And it is your Spirit which cries out within us,
>   longing to see this world
>   >   finally one.

We pray that we may let go
>   of all that keeps us from full union with your loving power
>   >   in creation.
We join our prayer with the prayer of all those
>   >   who have cherished this earth before us,
>   >   who have only apparently left us
>   >   >   for a while,
>   >   whose spirit calls us
>   >   >   to care for this earth
>   >   >   >   in new ways
>   >   >   >   in a new time in human history,
>   >   and who long to have us tell them our story
>   >   >   when we join them in the final banquet
>   >   >   of eternal life.

We make our prayer in the name of Jesus,
>   for it is through him
>   >   and with him
>   >   and in him
>   that all glory and honor are yours, Eternal Creator,
>   >   in the unity of the Holy Spirit,
>   >   >   now and forever. Amen.

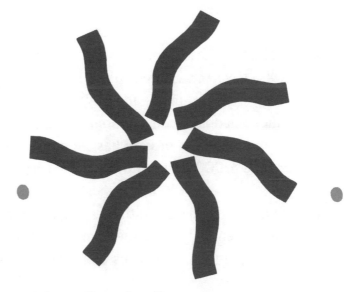

12. GOD'S GALAXIES

HOLY THURSDAY

BLESSING PRAYER

We are children of God,
    born of shooting stars
    and careening comets.

But we are also part of a particular people.
We have a history
    and a heritage.
We are borne on the shoulders of other co-creators.
We do not journey alone among these galaxies.

And so as we take up this bread and wine,
    the signs of the fruitfulness of this creation
    and of the labors of its peoples,
        we remember
        and we praise our God.

We remember all those special men and women
    who have contributed to the shaping
        of our unique identity,
    those people through whom
        the light of God has shone in a special way for us.
We trace the 6,000 years of our family story.

We remember the shining faith of Abraham and Sarah,
    strong enough to let them imagine in themselves
    a people more numerous than the sands of the seashore.

    And we remember the blazing comet
        called Moses and Miriam.

We celebrate psalmists
    so rich in insight and beauty
        that they can touch the depths of our own dream
          and pain
          and despair.

We join hands with Esther and Ruth
    and Isaiah and Joseph,
    and we dream with our mind's eye
        a great cloud of witnesses,
    each nameless,
    but each unique,
        stretching from the stars
        to this place and time.

We take our place with them,
    this unique gathering
    at this unique moment
    in this unique space,
and we sing the words of the prophet
in the presence of all this holiness:

Holy, holy, holy Lord, God of power and might.
Heaven and earth are full of your glory.
Hosanna in the highest.
Blessed is he who comes in the name of the Lord.
Hosanna in the highest.

But even this was not enough for our God.
And so we were given
    the person of Jesus
        in which to see what the fullness of creation,
        the fullness of holiness,
        the fullness of love,
            might mean.

We walk with him,
    and we celebrate those
        who found their own light by being with him.

We rejoice in a Samaritan woman
    who had the courage of her selfhood,
    who was not afraid to sit by a well
        and talk about God with this Jew,
        who came to recognize her desire for living water,
    and who was free to ask for it.
And who told others her good news.

We dine with Mary and Lazarus and Martha,
    with men and women
    who walked the roads of Galilee and Judea with him.

We celebrate the quiet steel
    of the star we call Mary,
        who knew in her bones
        that the mighty will be put down
        and the poor and lowly uplifted.

And we remember him
  in whom the light has overcome all darkness.
And we do
  as he has asked us to do:
    we offer ourselves
    as he offered himself.

He had gathered with his friends,
  much as we gather this night of remembrance.

He praised and blessed our God
  like one of his and our people.

Then he did the unique, the new thing.

He took the bread there on the table before him,
  and he broke it
    in his unique way,
  and he gave it to them as he said,
  "Take this and eat it.
    It is my body being given for you."

And then he lifted the cup
  and offered it to them as he said,
  "Drink from this, all of you.
    It is the cup of my blood.
    I will pour it out for you
      and for all on this earth.

When you remember me,
  you do the same."

And so with great joy we sing the praises of our God.

(Sung anamnesis.)

He went forth to do
      what he had promised.

He gave himself over into death.

But our God accepted his offering,
      blessed him with new life,
      and gifted us with his life,
          his light,
          and his power.

In that power we join in a special way
      with those with whom we share this life.

We pray together
      with all those people around our globe
          who have been transformed by his light
          and have become light
          and have become love
          by doing the deeds of justice and mercy and care.

We thank our God for those
      who walk ahead of us along the way,
          whose light illumines us.
Their star has passed through the orbit of our earth
      to its final place in the heavens.

So we do not even know them by name;
      we know only that their splendor has touched us.

Others' names are scratched in our hearts.

One day we will take our place with all of them
      when our life has traced its path across the skies.

They are all gathered with us
     in the cosmic body of this Jesus
         who has become the Christ,
         the fullness of God's glory.

Through him,
     with him,
     and in him
         all glory and honor are yours,
           our God,
              for ever and ever. Amen.

CONCLUDING RITUAL

Leader:

We are God's children, expressions of love, destined to be love in this world. And what does it mean to be love?

First Reader:

Jesus said: "From now on, I tell you, I shall not drink wine until the day I drink the new wine in the kingdom" *(Luke 22:15-18).*

Second Reader:

He said to them: "When I sent you out without purse or haversack or sandals, were you without anything?" "No," they said. He said to them: "But now if you have a purse, take it; if you have a haversack, do the same; if you have no sword, sell your cloak and buy one, because I tell you these words of Scripture have to be fulfilled in me; He let himself be taken for a criminal. Yes, what scripture says about me is even now reaching its fulfillment" *(Luke 22:35-37).*

1st Reader:

He then left to make his way as usual to the Mount of Olives,
with the disciples following. When they reached the place he said
to them: "Pray not to be put to the test." Then he withdrew from
them, about a stone's throw away, and knelt down and prayed
(Luke 22:39-41).

2nd Reader:

"I tell you most solemnly, unless a wheat grain falls on the ground
and dies, it remains only a single grain; but if it dies, it yields a rich
harvest. Those who love their life will lose it; if you hate your life
in this world you will keep it for eternal life. Now sentence is
being passed on this world; now the prince of this world is to be
overthrown. And when I am lifted up from the earth, I shall draw all
to myself" *(John 12:31-32).*

Leader:

We are still on only one planet in this vast cosmos. But we are also
the unique children of our God, trying to learn what it means to be
love. Let us bless one another as we continue on our journey, as Jesus
shows us the way. I invite you to turn to your neighbor, extend your
hands in blessing, and receive blessing in return.

EASTER

GREETING

The grace and peace and joy of the Risen Christ be will all of you.

All: And also with you.

We gather on this joyful morning with the new life and beauty of this creation almost overwhelming us, and we praise and adore our God.

On Thursday evening we began our celebration by going out among the stars and looking "back" into this tiny blue earth, and we prayed over what it means that we are God's children, manifestations of love and holiness simply by the fact that we are. And then we were given the food and the life, and the death, of Jesus to teach us what it means to be love.

Today we learn the fruit of love given over into death. We enter into the greatest surprise of all. Life overcomes death; hatred is transformed by love; darkness does not prevail.

And so let us gather ourselves in prayer together:

> Our brother Jesus,
>> your transformation has been enacted,
>> it has been brought to completion.
> Just as you said it would.

> But you also said that if you were lifted up
>> you would draw all things to yourself.

That drawing is taking place
    even now,
        in us
        and in the whole of creation.
Give us your eyes to see it,
your mind to understand
    and appreciate it,
your heart to rejoice in it.
And let the joy it brings us spring up in us
    as a fountain of energy
    to do the deeds of truth
        and justice
        and peace
        and love
    which delight and give glory to our God
        now and forever. Amen.

BLESSING PRAYER

Our loving God,
    it is right that we praise you.

Your creative energy has never ceased to expand in this creation.
    It moved through Adam and eve.
    It burst forth in the song of David
        and the wisdom of Solomon;
    It flashed in the courage of Esther
        and sustained the faithfulness of Job.
Even as we celebrate today,
    it emboldens Desmond Tutu and Dennis Hurley
    to raise their voices for the detained children of South Africa.
And it rushes through us, too,
    impelling us to cry out in blessing
    with the words of all the holy ones down through the ages:

Holy, holy, holy Lord, God of power and might.
Heaven and earth are full of your glory.
Hosanna in the highest.
Blessed is he who comes in the name of the Lord.
Hosanna in the highest.

Above all it continues to course
        through the flesh
        and sinews
                of the risen Jesus.

The world is not as we poor disciples had imaged it.
His death was not the end;
        and neither is ours.

His voice was not silenced,
his mission not stifled,
his prayer not left unheard;
        and neither are ours.

The life that was in him
and is now spilled out into us
        will not be dammed up;
it will reach the consummation
        you have willed for it.

And so we return to the table
        where he offers his life for us
        once more.
We take bread,
        as he took bread.
We sing your praise
        as he sang your praise.
And we offer ourselves
        as he offered himself.

We do his very own deed.

For we remember that he broke bread
     in his unforgettable way
and said to us:
     "Take this and eat it.
        This is my body,
        being offered anew
           for you."

And when the meal was finished
he took a cup of wine
and gave it to those who were with him,
and he said:
     "This cup is the new covenant;
        my blood poured out
           for you.
        Drink from it,
           all of you.
And then do as I have commanded you,
     as a memorial of me:
        love one another as I have loved you."

Lord, we do remember.

With this meal we are inserted into his life
     and his death,
     but also by your Spirit
        we are inserted into the mystery of his risen life.

You make us his body in the world.

And so we pray, not alone,
     but in union with all those
        joined with us in faith around our globe.

We pray for eyes to see
        beneath the appearances of this world
               to the transformation you are working.

We pray for hearts of flesh
        and human hands
               so that our touch and our work
               may be your touch, your work.

We pray that our church may turn
        from concentrating on the deaths of sin
               and find itself sustained by the miracle of life.

We know that we see but small fragments
        of your mystery unfolding.

And so we know that there are more than just ourselves here.
        Surrounding us are all those who go before us,
        our brothers and sisters
               who have passed through the veil that dims our vision
                   and hides the even more glorious mystery.
        We join our prayer with theirs
               even as we anticipate the day
                   when we will join them at that great table
                   which awaits us in your kingdom.

We pray in the body of Jesus,
               for it is through him
               and with him
               and in him
        that all glory and honor are yours, Eternal Creator,
               in the unity of the Holy Spirit,
                   now and forever. Amen.

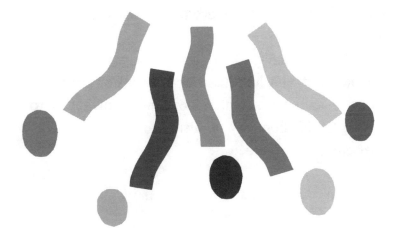

13. A SINGLE FABRIC

INVITATION

(In the center of the prayer space, a large basket is hung from the ceiling. Many ribbons or streamers, anchored in the basket, hang over the sides.)

We enter our worship space and symbolically claim and own our personal uniqueness — and our connectedness with the single fabric of creation.

We ask those in the front row to come forward quadrant by quadrant and take hold of two or three ribbons hanging from the basket in the center; then return to your places. First those from the north sector of the room, then east, south, and west.

Now we invite all those in the front row to turn and face those in the second row and give to each person a ribbon. If you need more ribbons to take care of everyone in the second row, just come back to the basket and take another.

Now we invite everyone to ask someone in front of you or next to you
to assist you in tying your ribbon around one of your wrists.

We were already one seamless fabric even before we tied ourselves
together symbolically. It's just that our finite vision promotes the
illusion of our separateness. Our ribbons are an invitation to enter
into prayer that the illusion may be dispelled, that we may come to the
truth of what and who we are.

And so let us join our minds and hearts in prayer.

Blessing Prayer

> Our divine,
>   loving,
>   creative Mother,
> there is but one energy
>   shaping and moving every last particle
>   of this vast universe:
>   your love ceaselessly exploding
>   in eternally unique embodiments,
>   each reflecting in a small way
>   — often hidden from our feeble vision —
>   some subtle hue or glint
>   or shade of the rainbow palette
>   that is your life poured out.
>
> Tonight we bless and praise you
> for our place in the long galaxy of creation.
>
> We celebrate the network of stars and planets
>   within which our tiny earth
>   brings forth its teeming forms of life.

We contemplate in awe
> the power you have given to us
> to bring all that beauty
>> to conscious reflection.

We rejoice in the words and colors,
> the sounds and smells cast by all the human artists
>> — famous and hidden —
> who have shaped the earth
>> into beautiful re-creations
>>> of you.

We sing our rich entanglement
> in the stuff of prophets and paupers,
>> of nomads and city-builders;
we proclaim our common story
> with fallen evangelists
>> and greedy munitions merchants,
> and spineless politicians
>> and addicts of all sorts.

But above all,
> our tender Father,
we kneel before the mystery of your unique Word,
> the one you declared all-pleasing,
>> Jesus of Nazareth become
>>> through death and rising
>>> the anointed and anointing of all creation.

In the conscious presence of this holiness
> we might be tempted to stand mute.

But you have made us to sing.
> And so we dare,
we dare to chant the song of your prophet:

Holy, holy, holy Lord, God of power and might.
Heaven and earth are full of your glory.
Hosanna in the highest.
Blessed is he who comes in the name of the Lord.
Hosanna in the highest.

Jesus sang your praise in deeds;
     he touched lepers
     and he disarmed over-zealous disciples,
     he drank with sinners
     and he blessed wedding banquets.

In words he painted our imaginations
     with sparrows
     and widows
     and fools
     and swine.

He breathed
     and spat
     and sweated
     and bled.

And finally, when he had apparently exhausted the ways
     of mirroring your love,
     he found another.
He looked into the face of death —
     the death of betrayal by one he had called friend,
     the death of a broken body,
     the death of final abandonment
          by you —
     and he said yes.

And he gave himself at the table —
     as he does this night.

He took bread;
he blessed you;
he broke the bread open.
He said: "This is my body."

He took a cup of wine in his hands.
He said: "This is my blood.
    It is a new covenant,
      poured out for all.
Take this food;
take this drink.
    Whenever you gather,
        do these same things
            and remember me."

Let us proclaim in great awe
    this mystery of our faith.

(Acclamation.)

In the power of his free passage into death,
in the incredible gift of his resurrection,
in the gushing forth of his Spirit,
we are able to stand in your presence this night,
    our creator
    and redeemer
    and sanctifier,
and to claim our creaturehood in prayer.

We pray for the whole of this lovely creation,
    that its full potential to reveal and praise you
    may not be diminished
      by our greed and thoughtlessness,
      our fear and violence.

We pray in a special way for those we call "church",
>   those who share our unique heritage
>>   and faith
>>   and journey.

We pray particularly this night
for those sisters and brothers of ours
>   around our earth
>>   who are
>>   at this moment
>>   icons of Christ
in confronting forms of death
>   we can scarcely imagine.

We pray for those called to leadership,
>   in our world
>   and in our church,
>>   that they may hear the voices
>>>   crying out for peace and justice.

And we pray for ourselves,
>   that we may be those voices.

Our prayer is joined with the chorus of all creation,
>   which will one day be a wedding banquet
>>   at which we will realize
>>>   that we are seated with you,
>>>   face to face.

We pray in the name
>   and in the power of him
>>   whom you have anointed,
>   Jesus Christ.

<blockquote>

For it is through him
>   and with him
>   and in him
> that all glory and honor are yours, Eternal Creator,
>   in the unity of the Holy Spirit,
>   now and forever. Amen.

</blockquote>

After the Common Meal

<blockquote>

Our creator God,
> you have never failed
>   to feed us along our journey.

We thank you
>   for the life of Jesus
>   shared among us this night.

Continue to hold us
>   within the supporting web of your creative love,
>   for without you
>   we sink into nothingness.

Let us know you
>   in the dance of our common life,
>   which we continue with Jesus the Christ
>   forever and ever. Amen.

</blockquote>

Conclusion of the Ritual

We untie our ribbons,
>   for they are only symbols.

We know now
that we are bound
by the love Christ poured out for us.

Let us share our peace
and continue our feast.

Mazeltov!

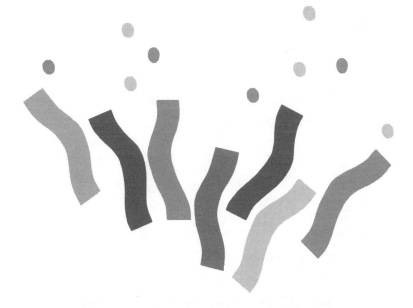

14. CEREMONY OF NEW FIRE

(The ceremony begins in a darkened room, or outside after dusk.)

Inviter: People of the Lord! Come!
Why do you sit in darkness?
Our God is bringing us light.
You'll see each other's faces.
You'll see that you are not alone.

Responder: I don't know.
It still looks dark to me.
We might not make it.
Here it's at least secure,
even though it's dark.
If we just stick together here
we might even make our way back —
to the way it used to be.

Inviter: Neighbors!
              Fellow pilgrims!
              Come on out!
              The flames will soon be dancing
                    and playing in the sky.
              Our God is inviting us
                    to play and dance
                          on her earth.

Responder: Actually, it might be fun.
              (Pause.)
              It sounds pretty irresponsible to me, though.
              Why, I've got meetings to go to,
                    and projects to organize.
              If I take time to play around the fire,
                    who will write all those letters to Congress?
              (Pause.)
              Then again,
                    sometimes I just get tired
                    and wonder what I'm really accomplishing
                          by all the work anyway.

Inviter: Friends?
              You whom Jesus calls friends.
              Come on!
              It's only a fire,
                    it's not the full dawn yet.
              But it's real.
              And our God has provided it for us.
              (Pause)
              It's free, you know.

Responder: I think I'm beginning to make out the pattern.
Darkness,
struggle,
no way out —
     and then she surprises us.
The pattern is all there;
I can feel it written right in our bones.
Maybe we might trust it
     one more time.

Inviter: There's even water to refresh you, you know.

Responder: I thought you'd never mention that.
That does it.
Where do we go?

Inviter: Come then,
all of you,
     to the fire that will warm us
        as we wait for the full dawn,
     to the water that will refresh us
        on the way.

BLESSING AT THE FIRE

May the God who continually fashions the earth that we are
   in-spirit that earth with creative energy,
      that our bodies may perform the deeds
        of mercy and care;

May the God who breathes air and life into our dry bones
      rush within the caverns of our lungs,
      that our voices may utter the piercing cry
         of peace;

May the God who is fire
      enkindle in our hearts passion,
         that we may have the courage
            to do the dangerous deeds
            of justice;

And may the God who bathes and refreshes this creation
      and all of us with water,
         empower us
      for the soothing deeds of love,
   our Creator and Redeemer and Sanctifier.
         Amen.

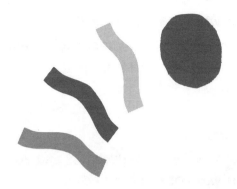

15. RESURRECTION: THE UNEXPECTED

GATHERING

We gather today much as the disciples on that first Easter: still with
questions, still unsure, but drawn back once more. We are still being
called to the table. But now our host is the one who has known death
and overcome it. His flesh bears the marks of the violent ones but is
now transformed. All is transformed! If we could but see it.

And so I say to you:
the grace and the peace and the joy of the Risen Christ be yours.

BLESSING PRAYER

> Our indwelling Creator,
> > it is our privilege,
> > our holy calling,
> > our great joy,
> > > to bless your name at all times, in all seasons.
> On this day above all days we celebrate
> > the tender way you continue to surprise us
> > > with your love.

When we contemplate the fullness of your life
    all by yourself,
        it was not to be expected
        that you should choose to bring into being
            this world of limited, transitory beings.

All: It happened.

And when we sinned
    and placed a barrier between us and your holy love,
        it was not to be expected
        that you would tear down the wall between us.

All: It happened.

And when our people were suffering in exile,
    it was not to be expected
        that you would call forth a leader
        from among us
        to throw off the shackles of oppression.

All: It happened.

And when the armies of the enemy had us pinned
    against the bank of the river,
    it was not to be expected
        that you would open up a pathway
        for our freedom
        through those very waters.

All: It happened.

And when our people were relegated
    to a back-water of human history,
    it was not to be expected
    that you would take flesh
        in the womb of a Jewish woman
        in a forgotten village.

All: It happened.

And so we sing the glory of your repeated surprises of new life,
with the whole of this unexpected creation:

> Holy, holy, holy Lord, God of power and might.
> Heaven and earth are full of your glory.
> Hosanna in the highest.
> Blessed is he who comes in the name of the Lord.
> Hosanna in the highest.

Finally we bless you for your greatest surprise.
For Jesus.

We bless you that he continually broke out of the tiny boxes
in which even his own holy people tried
to constrain your redeeming power.

It was not to be expected that a Jewish man
would sit by a well with a Samaritan woman,
that he would ask her simply to quench his thirst
with a drink of water.

All: It happened.

It was not to be expected that a tradesman
from Nazareth
would stand in the synagogue
and proclaim that the prophecy of liberation
was fulfilled in his flesh.

All: It happened.

It was not to be expected
that the Messiah
would heal on the Sabbath
and declare that the Sabbath itself
was less important than human life.

All: It happened.

And it was not to be expected
>   that in the face of his own destruction
>   and the desertion of his trusted friends
>   he would respond
>   by offering them his own body and blood
>   as the food and drink of everlasting life.

All: It happened.

He ate the meal of his people with them.
He sang their sacred songs and told their ancient story.
Then he took the bread on the table;
>   he blessed you, the all-holy One;
>   and breaking it,
>   he gave it to them.

He said: "Take this, all of you.
>   Take it and eat it.
>   This is my body. It is being broken and given for you."

And then he took the cup of wine.
He blessed you
and he gave it to them with the words,
>   "Share this cup among you.
>   It is the cup of my blood.
>   It seals a new and irrevocable covenant,
>   for you and for all people.

When you gather as my holy people,
do these same things in memory of me."

(Acclamation.)

After his murder
it was not to be expected
>   that his life might continue.

All: It happened.

It was not to be expected that
    when the women came to care for his dead body
      he would be gone;
that he would greet his cowering disciples with the command
    not to be afraid,
    that his own peace would be with them;
      or that he would cook fish for them
        by the side of the lake.

All: It happened.

And finally it was not to be expected
    that he would pour into them
    and us
    the very Spirit which animated his own body,
      so that they and we might do the things he did —
      and even greater.

All: It happened.

Down through the ages ordinary men and women
    like us
have broken open the shell of false traditions
    and poured out the incredibly rich wine
      of their own blood.
They have contested Roman emperors
    who laid claim to their own divinity,
    and white supremacists
      who tried to deny black people
        their fundamental humanity.

They have kissed lepers
    and opened closed human minds;
    they have imaged you in art
      beautiful beyond the telling
    and songs the angels cannot reach.

They have visited prisoners
     and comforted widows
     and sheltered the homeless
     and washed each other's feet.

And they have transformed hardened hearts.

It was not to be expected, but —

All: It happened.

As we hold up before you the offering of Jesus
     we do so in union with this great throng
         of compassionate witnesses
             down through the ages.

We do so
     in the hope
     and the confidence
         that you will continue to surprise us
            in our day
            and our time
            and in our very bodies,
until we take our place
     once and for all
         with the risen Lord,
         the Christ of this creation.

For it is through him
     and with him
     and in him
that all glory and honor are yours, Eternal Creator,
in the unity of the Holy Spirit, now and forever. Amen.

16. GOD IN OUR HISTORY: THE WALL

INTRODUCTION

(Replace dated events with appropriate contemporary events.)

We gather again in the presence of the God of this incredible creation, the God of our human history. Once more we place ourselves within the unfolding life of the Christ. We come in the confidence that through the Spirit who prays within us Christ will reveal to us yet once again the mystery of our magnanimous God.

Each year the story of our lives unfolds a little more. Year after year, God invites us into the depths of our common calling. We are one people. And so we unscroll together the page of our collective history in order to discern there what the finger of our God has written in these 365 days. We do so in the hope of learning to read the divine plan just a little better. In the hope of knowing better who we really are. For what happened in our world happened *to us.*

We try now to recall just how it was in our world during the past year, before our potter-God went down into the potting shed and decided to smash some old wares. To make new things. We thought we knew our world and how it worked.

(Pause.)

Chronology I   *(Three readers.)*

☐ June 3rd, 1989: After weeks of peaceful student protests in Tiananmen Square, government troops fire indiscriminately on the protesters; hundreds, perhaps thousands, are killed. On the same day in Teheran the Ayatollah Khomeini dies.

☐ June 4th: In the first free multi-party elections in Poland the Communist Party is overwhelmingly defeated by Solidarity.

☐ August 19th: General Wojciech Jaruzelski approves the first non-Communist government in Poland in over 40 years.

(Pause.)

Responsory Reading

(Select a New Testament reading.)

Chronology II

☐ September 30th, 1989: By agreement of the governments of East and West Germany East German refugees in Prague and Warsaw are allowed to leave for the West. Within two weeks more than 45,000 arrive in West Germany.

☐ October 7th: Recognizing that it has lost all power, the Hungarian Communist Party disbands.

☐ November 9th: The East German government lifts travel restrictions. The Berlin Wall is opened. The people dance on the Wall, even as they begin to dismantle its blocks.

(Pause.)

RESPONSORY READING

(Select a New Testament reading.)

CHRONOLOGY III

☐ November 29th: The Communist Party of Czechoslovakia loses its constitutional guarantee of retaining power.

☐ December 1st: The Communist Party of East Germany gives up its constitutional guarantee of retaining power.

☐ December 20th: In an effort to capture Manuel Noriega the United States invades Panama. Innocent Panamanians are killed, in numbers still uncounted.

☐ December 22nd: After a week of protest suppressed by government violence, Nicolae Ceaucescu of Romania is driven from power in a popular uprising.

☐ Christmas Day, 1989: A tribunal finds Nicolae Ceaucescu and his wife Elena guilty of crimes against the people of Romania. They are executed by firing squad immediately.

(Pause.)

RESPONSORY READING

(Select a New Testament reading.)

CHRONOLOGY IV

☐ January 4th: Manuel Noriega surrenders to United States troops.

☐ February 7th: Leaders of the Communist Party in the Soviet Union agree to a multi-party government system.

☐ February 11th: After 18 years in prison Nelson Mandela goes free. He puts himself at the disposal of the leadership of the African National Congress.

☐ February 26th: Violetta Chamorro is elected president of Nicaragua, ending 10 years of Sandinista rule.

(Pause.)

RESPONSORY READING

(Select a New Testament reading.)

Leader: Barriers are removed.
        Openings created.
        People able to touch one another, to embrace again.

        But will they? will we?

        Our world stands on uncertain ground.
        This place is new.
        No old enemies to blame.
        Freedom is so much more demanding than tyranny.
        We have been let out of the prisons of old assumptions —
        and into a new open space where we will be asked inexorably:
                now what do you want?

What do you believe?
What kind of a world will you fashion?
What kind of people will you choose to be?

(Community processes to an assembly room. They find it divided by a "wall" of cardboard boxes painted grey.)

Reader: What is this? What do these stones mean?
I thought we were here to celebrate
liberation from barriers — who has built yet more?

Presider: Yes, we celebrate.
But we do so as an ancient people, old enough
and wise enough
to know that there are still other walls
that must come down,
other prison cells
that must be opened before we can embrace.

We place ourselves before the barriers
as Jesus stood before them.
We hear how he wrestled with the question:
how to remove them?

Reader: *(Jesus' temptations in the desert: Matthew 4:1-11.)*

Presider: As we sit with Jesus at table
we are confronted with the walls that remain,
the divisions within our world
and within our own spirits.
We face the painful truth
that they are barriers of our own making.

READING

(Select a New Testament reading.)

Compassion is a sign of the presence of the divine.
Jesus calls us to
    "be compassionate as your Creator is compassionate."
Compassion is interdependence.
    And the universe is already there.

Our work is to enter into that truth
and in the strength of that consciousness
        to struggle at building human institutions
        that encourage and support conscious interdependence.

To exercise compassion
        it is not enough to be conscious of our interdependence;
we must struggle to live in interdependence
        with one another
        and with creation.

(People are then invited to come to the well; tell the group the particular "stone of separation" they want to work to remove, and then take one of the blocks away.)

BLESSING PRAYER

At the table
        we learn from Jesus
        how the stones are to be removed.
First, last, and always
        we must stand in worship and thanksgiving.

("Holy, holy, holy" is sung, while the table of gifts is set.)

> Holy, holy, holy Lord, God of power and might.
> Heaven and earth are full of your glory.
> Hosanna in the highest.
> Blessed is he who comes in the name of the Lord.
> Hosanna in the highest.

Then we must do as he did,
    offer ourselves.

Jesus took the bread in their midst.
He gave it to them
    and to us.
And he told us what it really was.
He said, "Take this and eat it.
    It is my body.
    It is being given over into the hands of death
        for you."

And then he took the cup of wine.
He said, "Drink of this, all of you.
    It is my blood.
    It will be poured out for you,
    as the sign of a new and irrevocable covenant,
    as the way our fractured world is to be made whole:
        love one another
        as I have loved you."

And so we worship our God,
    in the power of Jesus' self-surrender,
    in the power of his Spirit
        within us.

We join our prayer with the whole of his body,
>   with the whole Christ;
>   and in a special way
>   with those joined to us in faith
>   this night
>   around our globe.

We pray that we may be loosed from the bonds
>   which hold us from one another
>   and from this holy earth.

We pray that we may learn more deeply
>   what it means to offer our bodies up
>   to the deeds of love
>   and care
>   and justice
>   and peace-making.

And we pray in the consciousness that we are not alone here,
>   for we are one body with a great cloud of witnesses
>   who have loved as he loved
>   and whose strength emboldens us
>   to believe that we can do the same.
Some we have known by name,
and we call on them to be with us in a special way this night.

(Pause)

We make our prayer through Christ
>   and with him and in him,
>   for only in that way is our God glorified,
>   this night and all nights
>   till time is no more. Amen.

A BAPTISMAL RE-COMMITMENT

(After a series of readings.) We began our time together by recalling
our common history of this past year. We saw our God remove walls
we had thought impossible to breach. Today we have probed yet
deeper into the recesses of our past, to see the compassionate hand of
our God present from the very beginnings of our life on this star. I
call you now, with this renewed understanding of who we really are,
to renew our common commitment:

> Do you promise
> that you will commit your human energies
> to work along side those who strive to remove the walls —
>   of whatever kind and no matter who initiated them —
>   which divide humans from one another?

> Do you promise
> that you will also work to remove any barrier
> between the human family
>   and the lovely earth our God has given to us
>   as a home to be cherished and reverenced?

> Will you commit yourself
> to that most difficult pilgrimage of all,
> the effort to bring to consciousness
>   the walls within your own heart
>   which keep you from bringing to our common mission
>   all the good gifts
>   with which our God has uniquely endowed you?

> Then I promise you the courage
>   and the support and the loving touch
>   of the Risen Lord.

Greeting

We gather today with all the rich experience of God's creative Spirit in
our hearts. We have seen our God at work in the story of this holy
creation, removing one by one the walls by which we would hide from
the fullness of life. And once again we are being called to the table.
But today we are aware more than ever that we dine with the Risen
Christ, who has shown us through his passage through death to life
how we are to remove the walls which still imprison us. There are no
walls within the Cosmic Christ — if we could but see it.

> And so I say to you:
> the grace and the peace and the joy of the Risen Christ
>   be with you!

17. Doorway To Otherness

Reflections and Readings

(In a gathering space separate from dining area.)

Leader:
We gather today to worship our God together. So I invite you now to relax and slowly center yourself. We are surrounded by the loving power of our Creator, sustaining and holding the universe and everything in it in vibrant tension.

Feel the solid ground beneath your feet and body, sustaining you by resisting, limiting, being "other" — defining what you can do, and what you cannot do.

Let your eyes pass slowly from face to face around the room. Allow yourself to sense the differences, the otherness, of each one. Let yourself settle into the wonder of how little we really know one another. How can I really appreciate her story, or his, or theirs? How can he look at reality that way; how can she be so blind to what is so clear to me?

We let ourselves experience our estrangement. We allow ourselves to feel our absolute uniqueness. And we go even into the recesses of our own hearts, to be confronted by all the conflicting voices we carry within, telling us how we should feel, and what's really true: What's good for us. What a woman is. What a man is. Or what it means to be patriotic, or brave, or Christian — or holy.

Even if there were no one else here, we would have otherness enough to deal with.

Reflector:
Our world — *we* — have just experienced our latest spasm of war. Oh, we know all the tired old excuses for it, we've heard them for centuries. But can we learn?

How easy to blame it all on the militarists and the weapons merchants.

How comforting.

And how untrue to our own identity! For we belong to a people that knows in its very sinews that, if a loving God comes to save us in solidarity as a single people, it is a salvation from sin and violence which infests us *as* a people.

To make the militarists 'other' than ourselves is to perpetuate the same folly by which they had to make the Iraqis other in order to kill them.

If we are to be fully one with those who are the victims we must know our oneness with those who make the bombs.

We can be saved from war only at the cost of touching within ourselves our own inclination to violence. When the distance between myself and the other becomes too great I will be tempted either to seduce it to change and become a reflection of me or to remove it from my world by whatever means: the violence of absorption or the violence of destruction.

For to love it *as* other will cost me my life as I have known it.

What is it that I don't want to challenge me and the way I have put my world together? What is it that we try to suppress or re-shape or drown out lest it destroy the temple we have been building for all these years?

Leader:
Soon we will gather with "the others."
We will hear together how Jesus confronted the other.

But first we invite you in this smaller setting to help us by telling us of the otherness which most troubles you.

Who, or what, are the 'visitors' or aliens who enter your world, with whom you feel you must wrestle as Jacob did?

What makes you want to lash out? What is 'out there' that you find hardest to find somewhere in your own soul?

(Time for quiet sharing of the experiences of temptation to violence. After some time, a bell rings, calling smaller groups together.)

Leader:
Let us go to meet our sisters and brothers,
        to hear the story of Jesus,
        to walk with him into the otherness of Passover.

(In the worship space, a free-standing door and frame have been erected, through which participants pass on their way to their places at table.)

Presider:

   We came together as scattered individuals,
         each seeking the face of peace,
         knowing that the price of true peace
               is that we name the fears that live within us
               and control us
               and impel us to suppress and destroy the other:
                     the other person,
                     the other culture,
                     the other race,
                     the God who is the Other.

   And now we have passed again through another opening,
         being drawn once again to become church.
               One body,
               called to cherish our uniqueness and differences
                     as so many revelations of the God
                           who has made this creation other
                                 in order to love it.

   And we turn to him
         who is totally one with us
         and totally other,
               Jesus,
         to catch some small glimpse of how he faced the other
               in his life.

*[Four readers are stationed at the four corners of the worship space,
outside the circle of participants. They take turns proclaiming the brief
Gospel texts, pausing after each.]*

Reader 1: After hearing his teaching many of his followers said, "This
is intolerable language. How could anyone accept it?" Jesus was
aware that his followers were complaining about it and said, "Does this
upset you?" *(John 6:59-61)*

Reader 2: All the people were astounded and said, "Can this be the Son of David?" But when the Pharisees heard this they said, "The man casts out devils only through Beelzebul, the prince of devils" *(Matthew 12:23-24).*

Reader 3: The unclean devil shouted at the top of its voice, "What do you want of us, Jesus of Nazareth? Have you come to destroy us? I know who you are: the Holy One of God." But Jesus said sharply, "Be silent!" *(Luke 4:34-35)*

Reader 4: Not even his brothers, in fact, had faith in him *(John 7:6).*

Reader 1: Taking him aside, Peter began to rebuke him. "Heaven forbid!" he said. "No, Lord, this shall never happen to you." But Jesus turned and said to Peter, "Away with you, Satan! You are an obstacle in my path; the way you think is not God's way!" *(Matthew 16:22-23)*

Reader 2: The woman said to him, "I know that Messiah is coming and when he comes he will tell us everything." Jesus said, "I am he." At this point the disciples returned, and were surprised to find him speaking to a woman *(John 4:25-27).*

Reader 3: Large crowds would gather to hear him and to have their sickness cured, but he would always go off to some place where he could be alone and pray *(Luke 5:15-16).*

Reader 4: Once more such a crowd collected that they could not even have a meal. When his relatives heard of this, they set out to take charge of him, convinced he was out of his mind *(Mark 3:20-21).*

Reader 1: "You don't know what you are asking," Jesus answered. "Can you drink the cup that I am going to drink?"

They replied, "We can."

"Very well," he said, "you shall drink my cup." *(Matthew 20-22-23)*

Reader 2: "Why do you want to kill me?" *(John 7:14)*

Reader 3: It is a narrow gate and a hard road that leads to life; and only a few find it *(Matthew 7:14).*

Reader 4: "My God, my God, why have you abandoned me?" *(Mark 15:34)*

Presider:

The door is indeed narrow.

It costs our life to go through it.

It takes faith to believe that a loving God

could be there

for me

if I risk passing through.

[Presider goes to the door and names an "other" that is hard for her/him to deal with; asks the community for prayer; invites others to come forward and name a 'door' they fear to pass through. After some time, the presider continues:]

And so we pray:

Blessing Prayer

Creator God, we praise you and bless you.
It is your wondrous love
 which holds us
 and this teeming creation
  in being.

But even the richness of the universe
  was not enough for you.
You wanted to lead us deeper into your mystery
 and so you called us out of slavery in Egypt
  into freedom —
 which took the form of a desert.
You came to liberate us in the form of a Persian emperor
 whom we would have called a pagan.
Again and again your prophets challenged the ways
 by which we were tempted to tame your holy freedom.
Again and again you went down to your potter's shed
 and smashed our idols,
  throwing us into confusion
  in order that we might have even greater life.

Till finally you came once and for all to us
 through the yes of a young Jewish woman
  in the otherness of a back-water village.

We sing your praise with the whole of creation
 in the words of Isaiah:

  Holy, holy, holy Lord, God of power and might.
  Heaven and earth are full of your glory.
  Hosanna in the highest.
  Blessed is he who comes in the name of the Lord.

Hosanna in the highest.
And finally we bless you
in
and through
Jesus.

He faced all that pushes us to violence
but continually reached out in love.
He was misunderstood;
his words were twisted;
his friendship and trust were betrayed.
Yet he would not break even the most bruised reed.

In total trust of your fidelity
he set his face toward Jerusalem
and the narrowest door of all.

"Now is my soul troubled," he said.
"Shall I say, 'Father, free me from this hour?'
Yet it was for this hour that I came."

And taking the bread that lay before them he said,
"All of you, take and eat.
This is my body.
It is being given for you."

"And drink of this cup;
it is my blood being poured out
as an everlasting promise
that you will be able to love as I do.
And when you do this, remember me."

We do remember, loving God,
and we pray that the Spirit of Jesus
in this food and drink

may unlock the doors of fear in our hearts.
We pray for all those joined with us in his church
    around our world.

Open our eyes to see your face
    in places
    and cultures
    and people
        that are strange to us.

Open our ears to hear your voice
    in sounds
    and cries
        we do not understand.

Give us the courage to touch your loveliness
    in corners where we are tempted to see only
    ugliness
        to be erased
    and crookedness
        to be straightened out
    and cacophony
        to be drowned out.

Join us to the prayer of those
    who have passed through the narrow door
        of death.

Show us that their power is with us
    to pull us through all the narrow doors along our way,
until we are all finally
    on the other side
        together,
        with Mary
        and all the rest of our holy family.

We make our prayer
>   in the name
>   and the power
>   >   of Jesus
>   >   >   our Passover.

For it is through him
>   and with him
>   and in him
>   >   that all glory and honor are yours,
>   >   Eternal Creator,
>   >   >   in the unity of the Holy Spirit,
>   >   >   now and forever. Amen.

18. EASTER: THE DOOR HAS BEEN OPENED

GREETING

As we gather, we recall our fears of the potential for violence within each of us. Having named our fears, we passed through a door and we became church, committed to helping each other to become people of peace.

And we know the price, as we recall how Jesus passed through the narrow door of death.

Today we gather in great joy because we know once more that the offer is accepted. Death is overcome, and with it our fear of being cut off from life and from our God.

And so I say to you: the grace and the peace and the joy of the risen Christ be with you!

All: And also with you.

A BAPTISMAL RE-COMMITMENT

Jesus has gone before us and passed through the narrow door of igno-
minious death, rejecting all recourse to violence. In his resurrection he
has become the fullness of life. On this most joyous of days he invites
us to renew our commitment to follow him through the narrow door.

And so I ask you:

☐ Do you commit yourself to approach through the door of faith,
refusing to be misled by appearances and always searching for the
deeper mystery of God at work in creation?

☐ Do you commit yourself to let go of false securities and pass
through the door of hope, relying on the infinite fidelity of our God in
the face of all that threatens your life?

☐ And do you commit yourself to pass through the door of love,
ready to pay the price for compassion with your brothers and sisters?

With our renewed commitment we become more fully joined to the
God of life and joy. Death can have no power over us; the veil of the
temple has been torn asunder and our God has become as near to us
as the welcome we extend to one another. Let us go in joy to the
table of our faithful God!

BLESSING PRAYER

Our loving
and continually creating God,
    it is our privilege
    and our calling
        to proclaim your name
        and your liberating love
            in every situation
            and every corner
                of this wondrous creation.

We do so in a special way on this day
    when we celebrate all the ways you have come
    to free us from our fear.

We were locked in exile in Egypt
    and you sent Moses and Miriam to lead us out.
All: The door has been opened.

We stood at the Red Sea with the enemy pressing upon us
    and you parted the waters.
All: The door has been opened.

We grumbled against you in the desert
    and you sent us manna.
All: The door has been opened.

We built you a temple
    and then we lost sight of what it was all about.
So you chose to enter the narrow womb
    of a young Jewish maiden
        to be born as one of us.
All: The door has been opened.

And so we sing the glory of your great deeds
of liberation,
with the whole of this lovely creation:

Holy, holy, holy Lord, God of power and might.
Heaven and earth are full of your glory.
Hosanna in the highest.
Blessed is he who comes in the name of the Lord.
Hosanna in the highest.

And we bless you for Jesus
and all he did and taught us in his life.

He had to pass through the door of temptation
to discover the meaning of his own calling as Messiah.
All: The door has been opened.

People with smaller vision,
including his own family,
wanted to imprison him in their narrow world-view
by teaching him
who he could talk to
(but he chose to travel about with women)
and who he could eat with
(but he chose to eat and drink with sinners)
and the deed he was forbidden to do on the Sabbath
(but he chose to heal the broken).
All: The door has been opened.

And Peter said he should not be put to death.
But he chose to pass through that narrowest of doors.

On the threshold of that doorway
he gathered with his friends
and celebrated the meal of their people.

He named his fear
>> but trusted in you,
>> and he gave himself over.

He took the bread and wine on the table,
gave thanks to you,
and said to them,
>> "Take this and eat it;
>>> it is my body,
>>> given into death for you.
>> And drink of this;
>>> it is my blood
>>> being poured out for you.
>> Remember me
>>> when you do these things
>> and let your hearts not be troubled with fear."

We remember how he went into death
>> in reliance on your faithfulness,
and we celebrate the victory you bestowed on him.
>> He is risen!
All: The door has been opened.

And he has poured out his Spirit into our hearts
>> so that we need not fear even death. Truly,
All: The door has been opened.

And so in the power of that Spirit
>> we celebrate your love
>> with all those in communion with us this great day.

We pray,
>> and we hope,
that our church community will increase the measure of hope
>> in our world;

that it will help to open doors for those
who are locked
in fear and hopelessness,
in cynicism and disbelief,
in selfishness and isolation.

And we draw strength in the realization
that our prayer is joined with the prayer of those
for whom the victory is complete
because they have entered through the final door
and await us at that last table in your kingdom.

We bless you
together with Jesus
who has passed through death
to the fullness of life.

For it is through him
and with him
and in him
that all glory and honor are yours, Eternal Creator,
in the unity of the Holy Spirit, now and forever. Amen.

19. BLINDNESS AND UNVEILING

GREETING

May the peace and the joy and the vision of the risen Christ
be with you!

As we gather today, we continue to pray that we might appreciate our
blindness and our need for the transforming power of the Lord to
enable us to see our world with God's eyes. On the night before he
died, Jesus took us to the table, and he asked how long he must be
with us until we catch on: that those who really see him see God.
And then he led us through the veil and into the mystery of weakness
and public humiliation and death.

Try as we may, we can't really re-live what his disciples went through
in those days: the utter irrationality of it, the loss of all bearings and
meaning, the loss of their whole world.

But our God is above all faithful. Promises are kept; the word that
came forth from the heavens like rain does not return empty. Today
we have new life. And new eyes. And so let us join our hearts in a
new prayer of adoration and blessing and thanksgiving:

Ever living, ever creating God,
>   you have taken us inside the mystery of your life
>>   in Jesus Christ.
With his Spirit we bless you.
And we pray
>   that you will continue to broaden and deepen our vision
>   until one day we realize fully
>>   how much you delight in this creation of yours
>   and choose to live your life within it.
Then we will give you the glory that belongs to you,
>   in Jesus and the Spirit, forever and ever. Amen.

BLESSING PRAYER

>   How right it is,
>   how just and fitting
>>   that we should praise you constantly,
>>>   our ever-present,
>>>   ever-creating God.
>   We are surrounded by your glory.
>   In the ever-shifting dance of earth
>>   and air
>>   and fire
>>   and water
>   we are given glimpses of the inexhaustible richness
>>   of your own life.

All: We are surrounded by your glory.

>   In galaxies
>   and quarks
>   and black holes
>>   you draw us beyond our small horizons
>>>   into your infinity.

All: We are surrounded by your glory.

In the play of light
and darkness
in every culture
and race
we tumble within the kaleidoscope
of your beauty.

All: We are surrounded by your glory.

And even in the constant struggle
of our conflicting desires and ambitions,
in the pain we inflict on one another,
you urge us to keep searching
for the lines of your countenance,
for you are present even there.

All: We are surrounded by your glory.

Down through the ages
you gave light to seers
and tongues to prophets —
named and nameless —
that your people might learn your ways
and bequeath to us
who follow in their footsteps
the precious treasure of wisdom.

We join with them on this brand new day
in praising your holiness with the age-old song:

Holy, holy, holy Lord, God of power and might.
Heaven and earth are full of your glory.
Hosanna in the highest.

Blessed is he who comes in the name of the Lord.
Hosanna in the highest.

Above all, your glory is revealed in Jesus.
He knew all that is in the human heart.
He looked out at the crowds who followed him
        seeking miracles
and he saw their real hunger and need
        for a richer food than that.

He saw a Roman centurion,
        not as an oppressor
                but as a father
                whose son was sick.

He saw beyond the limited horizon
        of his own family
and made all those who do your will
        his brothers and sisters.

And in total trust in you,
        whom he called Abba,
        he faced his own death.

But before he entered upon that mystery
        he looked with love on his followers
        and left them the food and drink
                of his own life.

They sat at table
and prayed the prayers
and sang the songs of his people.

Then he did a most unexpected thing.

He lifted the bread before them in thanksgiving to you,
and he said to them:
>"Take this and eat it.
>It is my body given for you."

And in the same way he took the cup of wine
and said,
>"Drink from this, all of you.
>It is the cup of my blood
>>to be poured out for you,
>>the blood of a new covenant
>>>which will last forever.

As often as you do these things, remember me
>for I will be with you."

(Acclamation.)

And so we do remember.

We remember that he died,
>and rose from the dead;
>that he returned to you in glory,
>and poured out his Spirit
>>so that we might be his body
>>in this world.

We are joined with all the artists who challenge us to his vision
>in so many tones
>and shapes
>and songs
>>of disturbing beauty.

All: We are surrounded by your glory.

With those who belong to this same body as we do,
>who have taught us how to look at life itself
>by handing over their own lives in witness to his truth.

All: We are surrounded by your glory.

And finally with those
>whose daily deeds — and *needs* —
>>are the gentle breeze
>that reveals more than all the whirlwinds:
>>those who wash one another's feet
>>and share the pain of the sick
>>>and the lonely
>>>and the imprisoned.

Truly . . . *(together)* we are surrounded by your glory.

With this whole community of the risen Christ
we sing your praise.
>For it is through him
>and with him
>and in him
>>that all glory and honor are yours, Eternal Creator,
>>>in the unity of the Holy Spirit,
>>>now and forever. Amen.

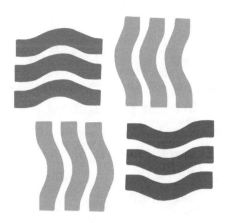

20. Our Persevering God

Greeting

To the God who was,
    the God who is,
    the God who will be;
the faithful God of our past,
    the loving God of our present,
    the provident God of our future;
all glory
    and adoration
    and blessing
through Jesus
    who has become the Christ
    and whose Spirit prays within us,
        this night and all days and nights
        till time is no more. Amen.

BLESSING PRAYER

It is our privilege,
and you have made it our birthright,
        our loving Creator,
to stand in your presence
        and bless you
        for your ever-faithful love.

Again and again down across the centuries
        you have come to us
        and showed your face to us
                even as we rebelled against you.

After our deliverance from slavery in Egypt
        we grumbled
        and cursed you;
You came to us in the guise of manna.

We turned to kings and arms
        because we could not trust in you;
You came to us in the form of prophets
        who reminded us of our story.
We were like bleached bones
                strewn about the valley of death
        and you promised to knit us together
                with new sinews.
When we became hard and uncaring
        you promised to give us hearts of flesh
                and compassion.
To this day we still dishonor and despoil this lovely garden
        in which you have settled us,
And you still give us stars to guide us
        and rainbows to delight us.

Your love has never ceased
      even in the face of our infidelity
      and unwillingness to allow ourselves to be loved.
And so we join the whole of your creation
in praising and celebrating your constancy, as we sing:

      Holy, holy, holy Lord, God of power and might.
      Heaven and earth are full of your glory.
      Hosanna in the highest.
      Blessed is he who comes in the name of the Lord.
      Hosanna in the highest.

But in order to reveal the full outpouring of your love
it was not enough that you should be present to us
      in all these signs.

You chose to clothe your own divinity
      in flesh like ours,
to live as one of us
      in the body and blood of Jesus.
In the pouring out of his own life
      and love
he would reveal who you are
      and how you love us.
He said,
      "I have come, not to be served but to serve,
      to give my life for many."
His family said he was mad,
      but he still set his face toward Jerusalem.
He said he had a baptism with which he was to be baptized
      — and longed that his hour should come.
His betrayer dipped food into the dish with him,
      but Jesus stayed at the table.
His disciples fought over who would have the first place,
      and he knelt and washed their feet.

And finally,
>   after singing the songs of his people,
he rose,
>   and did an unheard-of thing.

To join himself irrevocably with them
>   — and with us —
he took some bread and a cup of wine from the table
and said,
>   "Take this bread.
>   Eat it.
>   >   It is my body being given for you.
>   And drink, each of you, from this cup.
>   >   It is my blood being poured out for you.
>   This is the new covenant,
>   >   everlasting,
>   >   made fresh each time you do these things
>   >   and remember me."

(Acclamation.)

We remember;
we celebrate;
we believe.

And together with his Spirit we pray,
>   in a special way this night,
>   for all those knit together
>   >   as one flesh with us
>   >   in his body, the church.

We pray that we too may learn
>   how to be servants
>   >   of your creation
>   >   and its peoples.

That we may not turn aside
      from our journey to Jerusalem.
That we may stay at the table
      even with those who misunderstand
          and reject us.
That we may learn what it means,
      in this year,
      in *(your city);*
      in *(your state or country);*
      (Mention here countries and cities
      where there is conflict and need for cleansing.)
         that we are called to wash each other's feet.

We are one body at prayer this night
      with those who have gone before us
         in the pilgrimage of life. *(Pause for remembrance.)*
You gave them to us
      as revelations of your care.
They have taught us how to love,
      and the thought of joining them
         in the banquet in your kingdom
      is the final pledge of your unfailing faithfulness to us,
         hope as we continue on our journey.

And we are one with the whole of this wonderful universe
      giving witness to your unremitting care.

We pray
      with Jesus the Christ,
      and in him,
      and through him.
         For he gives you glory and honor,
            our faithful Creator,
            forever and ever. Amen.

A BLESSING OF NEW FIRE

Our creator God,
      your love is a flame.
It could not be contained and so you poured it out
      as the power which enlivens
      and sustains the whole of our universe.
The energy of the sun makes all life possible.

Today we ask your blessing on this small fire
      which partakes of that great energy.
May it make us continually aware of the blessing of life
      and the power you have given us to nurture it.
And may it be for us a reminder of that more thrilling fire,
      the Spirit of the risen Christ,
      which enables us to pour ourselves out
         in love and service of your beautiful creation
         and the lives of your people.

We pray in Jesus' name. Amen.

A BAPTISMAL RE-COMMITMENT

We have blessed the God of all the corners of creation,
>the God of earth and air and fire and water.
We have witnessed to the loving hand of our God
>in this universe
>>which sustains our life.

And so I ask you now
>in this brand new moment,
>>to join in a common commitment:

Do you promise
>that you will always strive to care for this lovely creation
in which we have been placed by our compassionate God,
>to be watchful stewards of its resources,
>and to speak out against the misuse of its treasures?

Do you promise
that you will seek the face of our God
>in each of your human companions,
>>trying to share their joys and their pain,
>>>their hopes and their fears?

Do you promise
that you will work always for just relationships,
>for that peace which is not complacency
>>but the product of cooperation,
>>the surrender of greed
>>>and jealous competition?

Then I promise you
    the courage
    and the support
    and the loving touch
        of the risen Lord.

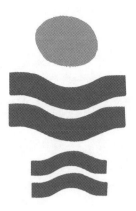

21. GOD GATHERING AND FEEDING

THIS IS MY BODY

BLESSING PRAYER

We come before you,
   our creator God,
   our saving God,
   our inspiriting God,
      in adoration and blessing.

From the beginning
you have placed us in this loveliest of creations
   as in a garden,
wherein we might share your own creative power,
   joining all manner of reality into unity and wholeness.

We were to shape
   but also be shaped by your cosmos;
we were to fashion and mold,
   but also ourselves be continually fashioned
   and molded
      by our common environment;

we were to be at home here,
> welcoming all
> and being welcomed by all.

And you would be with us and in us,
> always gathering, always feeding.

On this day above all we are aware
> that we have not been partners.

We have continually tried to master,
> and dominate,
> and subdue —
> > this earth,
> > and one another.

You alone have remained faithful to the covenant.

All: Always gathering, always feeding.

We tried to escape our bounds
and usurp your place,
> and what we created was Babel-babble,
> more fragments needing wholeness.

When our folly almost drowned us in the floods,
> you slaked our thirst for life
> and renewed our spirits
> > with an indelible rainbow in the sky.
> > You remained true to yourself.

All: Always gathering, always feeding.

Our ancestors built homes in which to reverence you —
> tents,

and tabernacles,
and temples —
> but always on our terms,
> to domesticate the energies of your Spirit,
> to claim it as our own
>> and shut others out.

In the name of the sacred.

But you sent us holy men and women,
> prophets to break open these poor shells
> and declare you once again the Potter
>> who will forever shatter our idols,
>>> again
>>> and again
>>> and again,
>> until we learn that all is holy.
In their words you were still with us.

All: Always gathering, always feeding.

When we made our world out of enemies
> and fear
> and mistrust,
and thought we could put it back together
> by horses
> and chariots
> and power politics,
you left us to our feeble resources
> so we might learn from the harsh school
>> of exile and slavery.

But then you sent us Moses and Miriam;
you drew us together in flight from the pharaoh;
you made us once again a people in the desert;

and when we cursed you for our hunger and thirst,
     you gave us manna.

All: Always gathering, always feeding.

We bless you for yourself.
We bless you for your constant fidelity.
And we bless you for our common story,
     the repeated renewal of your call to partnership.

We join our voices tonight to the many voices of the cosmos,
     each blessing you in its own unique way
          within the single song of adoration:

Holy, holy, holy Lord, God of power and might.
Heaven and earth are full of your glory.
Hosanna in the highest.
Blessed is he who comes in the name of the Lord.
Hosanna in the highest.

And finally you gathered all,
     you fed us all,
     through the life of Jesus of Nazareth.

His body given, his blood poured out.

He stood up in our midst
and declared what his mission was to be:
     the outpouring of your Spirit
          and his,
          a spirit which offers good news to the poor.

All: Always gathering, always feeding.

He stepped beyond the boundary dividing Jew and Samaritan,
    man and woman,
      slave and free.

He broke the taboos of his society,
      dining with tax-collectors
      and sinners.
He challenged the keepers of the law
who placed on others burdens they themselves would not carry.
  His touch soothed lepers
      and consoled widows
      and embraced children.

All: Always gathering, always feeding.

And then he sat at table one last time.
He was himself about to be shaped
      and molded
          by betrayal
          and emptiness,
to discover and reveal the fidelity of you, his Father,
      even in the ultimate dissolution of death.

And still he gathered,
still he fed.

After singing with them the songs of their story
      he rose
      and did a new thing.
He took the bread that lay before him;
he blessed it
and broke it,
and gave it to them, saying,
      "Take and eat this; it is my body, for you."

Then he took the cup of wine,
said a prayer of blessing,
and invited them to drink it together, saying,
      "This is the cup of my blood,
         poured out in a new and irrevocable covenant
            with you
            and with all.

When you gather, you do these same things.
      Feed one another
      and so remember me."

And so we do as we have been told.

In the power of his offering,
      of his unifying life, death, and resurrection
we come before you
      as a single people,
      a single cosmos,
         in blessing
         and adoration.

We join in a special way
      with all those we call "church"
and pray that we all may become better gatherers
      and nurturers;
that his freedom to die may enable us
      to let go of our tendency
      to build our lives at the expense of others.

Show us how to feed
and how to allow ourselves to be fed;
      to clothe and shelter,
      and allow ourselves to be clothed and sheltered.
Show us how to celebrate

when we see deeds of justice and liberation and courage;
and how to speak
    without self-righteousness
    when we must confront discrimination and violence.

Give us the courage to look at ourselves
    with the same mirror we put before others.

We are not alone here, Lord.
Part of our body is already fully gathered and being fed
    at your heavenly banquet.

Join us to all those who held us together
    and nurtured us
        while they were on their journey
            to you. *(Pause for memory of the dead.)*

We bless you with all of them,
    in the name and power of the risen Christ,
        for it is through him and with him and in him
    that you are blessed and praised,
        our loving God,
            forever and ever. Amen.

AT THE END OF THE MEAL

"I will strike the shepherd and the sheep shall be scattered."
"And leaving him they all fled."
Why did they have to put that into the Gospels?

Scholars propose the thesis that when we're searching for the historical facts in the Jesus story we can be reasonably sure we are in touch with the original reality when we read pieces that the early disciples would have found embarrassing, that they would have wanted to conceal in propagating the Good News. As we continue on the journey with

Jesus today and tomorrow we must also acknowledge our solidarity with those first disciples. It is only through the prism of their confusion and disillusionment that the full light of appreciation for the meaning of the resurrection can dawn on us. Only if we know the extent of our fragmentation can we appreciate the gift of God's gathering. Only the truly hungry can relish God's food; only the truly thirsty will savor the Lord's rich wine.

Let us pray:

You have gathered us and fed us richly this day,
      our generous God.
We thank you and we bless your name.
       As we are sent out into our many worlds,
           make us more worthy bearers
           of the good news of your faithfulness to your promise
           to be with us always.
This we ask in the name of him who is its perfect fulfillment,
      Jesus Christ, our Lord and Brother. Amen.

DO THIS IN MY NAME

BLESSING PRAYER

O wondrous,
magnanimous God!

On this most special day,
on this day of your most surprising self-revelation,
    it is our privilege
        to come into your presence
           in praise
           and blessing.

This beautiful creation had no right to exist.

There did not *have* to be snow-capped peaks
and captivating crocuses.
    Nor mighty whales
    or the oceans to cradle them;
        cypresses and mountain goats,
        snails and orchids,
        dinosaurs and tumbleweed. But —
your love could not be contained.

And so you shaped a cosmos.
You opened your hand
    and scattered planets
    and comets
    and stars
        like a child
        playing at jacks.

But you were not content to enjoy this panorama.
You wanted beings
> of spirit
> and heart
> and creativity
>> like yourself
> to share it.

All: Your love could not be contained.

And you entrusted your vision
> to Abraham and Sarah,
> to Isaac and Rebecca,
> to Jacob and Rachel,
> and Moses and Miriam.

They were to keep watch over your promise that,
> in spite of barrenness
> and infidelity
> and deceit
> and arrogance,
>> you would make your people as numerous
>> as the sands on the seashore.

All: Your love could not be contained.

You word of promise was twisted;
it was distorted;
it was turned inside out
> to hide injustice
> and conquest
> and avarice.

But it remained
> your word,
> your promise,
> your fidelity.

It was a seed sown that would not remain locked in death,
    gentle rain which would soak the rocky soil
        until it could not but bear fruit.

All: Your love could not be contained.

Until at last it rested in the womb of a Jewish girl
and was pushed forth
    as human flesh,
    as the body of Jesus of Nazareth,
        destined to become the Christ of the universe.

All: Your love could not be contained.

Your promise is alive in us this day,
    impelling us to live with the life of his Spirit.

So we join the whole of this magnificent cosmos
    in blessing and praising you
    in the words of the prophet
        who could only exclaim in awesome wonder:

        Holy, holy, holy Lord, God of power and might.
        Heaven and earth are full of your glory.
        Hosanna in the highest.
        Blessed is he who comes in the name of the Lord.
        Hosanna in the highest.

He came among us as one like us.
    As a Jew.
    As an ordinary tradesman.
    As from a village scorned for its rude ways.

Still . . . *(together)* your love could not be contained.

He came into a civic society
    that expected him to conform:

       to loath a Samaritan
       and disdain a prostitute and
       ignore a child.
Into a religious society
     that expected him to cultivate the surface
       so as to conceal the evils of the heart.
Into a political society
     that feared truth
       lest it shatter the idol of emperor-worship.

But these barriers could not hold him.
All: Your love could not be contained.

And so he crossed over every boundary.

He crossed every line.
     He gave himself into the hands of tax collectors
       and pharisees alike.
He endured the obtuseness of good-willed disciples
who tried to tell him the right way to go about his mission,
     and relatives
       who told him he was mad.

And finally his love brought him to the ultimate limit,
     to the dissolution of death.
We were to learn how strong your love for us really is.

They gathered at table on a holy night.
He washed their feet
     in the garb of a slave.
He sent his betrayer off
     without unmasking him before the others.

And he stopped a ritual meal to do a new thing.

He took the bread that lay before him,
blessed you, his Father,
     broke the bread
     and offered it to them, with the words,
         "Take this. It is my body.
         It is being handed over for you."
Then he took a cup filled with wine.
     And giving it to them, he said,
         "Take this. Drink it.
         It is the cup of my blood.
         This night it will be shed,
            for you and for all,
         As the sealing of an irrevocable commitment.
And as often as you do these very same things
         you will be proclaiming my death
         until I come again."

But death itself could not overcome your love.

You raised him from the dead
and gave him the name
     that is above every name:
         Lord and Christ.

And so we remember now.

We join ourselves to his act of total submission to you —
     in death,
     in rising,
     and in his ultimate glorification.
All: Your love could not be contained.

That love has burst all bounds,
     again and again
     down through the centuries.

It has freed holy men and women
      to challenge enslavements of every sort.
It has untied the tongues of poets
        and musicians
and challenged artists
     and architects
          to make the very stones transcend their limits
            in works of awesome beauty.
It has inspired humble people
     to soothe bodies ravaged with AIDS,
and helped countless parents
     to meet the painful challenge
        of guiding their children into adulthood.

It continues to dissolve the barriers that divide us,
     slowly molding us into a single people.
Even the barrier of death has been removed.

Those who have walked the journey before us
     are still one with us,
and those who will come after us
     are dressing for the procession.

Your love will not be contained
   until we are all joined
      at the single banquet table,
        singing the single song:
          through him, with him, and in him
            all praise and honor be yours,
              almighty Father,
                forever and ever.

     Amen.

22. THE GOD WHO DINES WITH SINNERS

Leader: Why are we assembled at this table? What brings me here? What brings you? What are we looking for? What do we seek on this particular night? We could, after all, each have dined alone. We could even have communed with our God. I invite you to pause for a moment to ask yourselves these questions, and then turn and share with one person the results of your reflections.

(After pause and sharing.)

Leader: Who is this Jesus with whom we dine? We listen to Matthew.

Reader 1: Jesus called his disciples and said to them, "I feel sorry for all these people; they have been with me now for three days and have nothing to eat. Do not send them away unfed; they might faint by the way." The disciples replied, "Where in this lonely place can we find bread enough to feed such a crowd?" "How many loaves have you?" Jesus asked. "Seven," they replied; "and there are a few small fishes." So he ordered the people to sit down on the ground; then he took the seven loaves and the fishes, and after giving thanks to God he broke them and gave to the disciples, and the disciples gave to the people. They all ate to their hearts' content; and the scraps left over, which

they picked up, were enough to fill seven baskets. . . . In crossing
to the other side, the disciples had forgotten to take bread with
them. . . . Jesus said to them, "Why do you talk about bringing no
bread? Where is your faith? Do you not understand even yet? Do
you not remember?" *(Matthew 15:32-16:9)*

Reader 2: "Is there anyone among you who would offer their children
stones when they ask for bread, or a serpent when they ask for a fish?
If you, then . . . know how to give your children what is good for
them, how much more will your heavenly father give good things to
those who ask?" *(Matthew 7:9-10)*

Leader: And so we come to the table of one who has compassion for
us, who does not want us to faint from hunger. We seek the bread of
life, and he says to us:

Reader 3: People can't live on bread alone; they need every word
that God utters. Don't ask anxiously, "What are we to eat? What
are we to drink? What shall we wear?" All these are things for the
heathen to run after, not for you, because your Father knows that
you need them all. Set your mind on God's kingdom and justice
before everything else, and all the rest will come to you as well"
(Matthew 6:31- 34).
Jesus said, "In very truth I know you have come looking for me
because your hunger was satisfied with the loaves you ate, not because
you saw signs. You must work, not for this perishable food, but for
the food that lasts, the food of everlasting life" *(John 6:26-27)*.

Leader: And so we come, seeking this food of eternal life. We
come, and we find other diners. Who are these people? With whom
do we dine?

Readers 1, 2, & 3 in unison: When Jesus was at table in the house,
many bad characters — tax-gatherers and others — were seated with
him and his disciples. The Pharisees noticed this, and said to his

disciples: "Why is it that your master eats and drinks with tax-gatherers and sinners?" Jesus heard them and said, "It is not the healthy that need a doctor, but the sick . . . . I did not come to call virtuous people, but sinners" *(Matthew 9:10-13)*.

Reader 1: "John came, neither eating nor drinking, and they say, "He is possessed. The Son of Man came eating and drinking, and they say, "Look at him! A glutton and a drinker, a friend of tax-gatherers and sinners!" *(Matthew 11:18-19)*

Reader 2: When Jesus came to the place, he looked up and said, "Zachaeus, be quick and come down; I must come and stay with you today." . . . At this there was a general murmur of disapproval. "He has gone in," they said, "to be the guest of a sinner" *(Luke 19:5, 7)*.

Reader 3: Someone was giving a big dinner party and had sent out many invitations. At dinner time the servants were sent with a message for the guests, "Please come, everything is now ready." They began one and all to excuse themselves. . . . The host was angry and said to the servants, "Go out quickly into the streets and alleys of the town, and bring me in the poor, the crippled, the blind, and the lame. . . . I want my house full. I tell you, not one of those who were invited shall taste my banquet" *(Luke 14:16-18, 21, 23-24)*.

Leader: And he tells us with whom we should share our table.

Reader 1: Then [Jesus] said to his host, "When you give a lunch or dinner party, don't invite your friends, your brothers or sisters, or other relatives, or your rich neighbors; they will only ask you back again, and so you will be repaid. But when you give a party, ak the poor, the crippled, the lame, and the blind, and so find happiness. For they have no means of repaying you" *(Luke 14:12-14)*.

Leader: For it is all pure gift.

Reader 2: Those who had started work an hour before sunset came forward, and were paid the full day's wage. When it was the turn of those who had come first, they expected something extra, but were paid the same amount as the others. As they took it, they grumbled against their employer: "These late-comers have done only one hour's work, yet you have put them on a level with us, who have sweated the whole day long in the blazing sun!" The owner turned to one of them and said, "My friend, I am not being unfair to you. . . . I choose to pay the last one the same as you. Surely I am free to do what I like with my own money. Why be jealous because I am kind?" *(Matthew 20:9-13a, 14-16)*

Leader: And finally he tells us what it all means.

Reader 3: During supper, Jesus, well aware that the Father had entrusted everything to him, and that he had come from God and was going back to God, rose from table, laid aside his garments, and taking a towel, tied it round him. Then he poured water into a basin, and began to wash his disciples' feet and to wipe them with the towel. When it was Simon Peter's turn, Peter said to him, "You, Lord, washing my feet?" Jesus replied, "You do not understand now what I am doing, but one day you will. . . . If I do not wash you, you are not in fellowship with me. . . . Do you understand what I have done for you? You call me 'Master' and 'Lord', and rightly so, for that is what I am. Then if I, you Lord and Master, have washed your feet, you ought to wash one another's feet. . . . If you know this, happy are you if you act upon it" *(John 13:2-7, 8b, 12b-14, 17)*.

Blessing Prayer

We know the one who comes to dine with us.

We know the meaning of his invitation and the food he shares.
And we have some small sense of who we are who are invited.

And so I say to you: The Lord is with you.

All: And also with you.

Lift up your hearts.

All: We have lifted them up to the Lord.

And let us give thanks and blessing to our God.

All: It is right to give God thanks and praise.

God of all compassion, we hunger for you.

> Ever since the dawn of creation
> > we have been drawn back to you,
> > > our source and origin.

> And never,
> > for even one second,
> > > have you left us untouched
> > > > by your presence
> > > > > and care.

> You gave us a garden of rich delight;
> > we would not accept your single limit,
> > > so you revealed to us our nakedness.
> We built a tower
> > to overcome our limits
> > and reach you
> > > on our terms;
> > and you washed the face of our earth
> > > with a flood,
> > and painted a rainbow in our sky
> > > as an unending sign of your covenant with us.

We sought your face in alien gods
        and human alliances
        and horses
        and weapons of war;
                and you responded with manna
                and parted seas
                and most unlikely liberators.

Because we were still going to reach you
        in our way,
                we had to taste exile
                        and slavery
                        and the shame of powerlessness;
        and you waited in the darkness of a Jewish girl's womb
                before meeting us
                with an intimacy beyond our wildest imagining.

Your love became flesh —
        our flesh —
                in Jesus of Nazareth.

We do this night what he told us to do.
We are gathered out of our isolation
        and we recall.

We remember.

We remember who you are,
and who we are,
and how he marries us to you
        irrevocably.

And in the telling,
the veil which shields us from the glory of all the holy ones
        dissolves.

In the power of his Spirit
       we are joined with the whole of creation
       as it sings the age-old hymn of your glory:

       Holy, holy, holy Lord, God of power and might.
       Heaven and earth are full of your glory.
       Hosanna in the highest.
       Blessed is he who comes in the name of the Lord.
       Hosanna in the highest.

He comes as one of us
and offers us unconditioned welcome —
       us as we are, in truth.
       This man eats and drinks with sinners.

All: This man eats and drinks with sinners.

He proclaims an invitation for us
          to receive sight
          and healing
          and truth
          and freedom
          and beatitude
          and liberation,
    and the world says:

All: This man eats and drinks with sinners.

He touches the eyes of a blind man
       and he begins to see;
he uses his own spittle to touch a man's tongue and ears
       so that he can speak and hear;
he touches the corpse of a widow's son
       and restores him to his mother's embrace.

And because he heals on the Sabbath,
 religious leaders say:

All: This man eats and drinks with sinners.

 He upsets the keepers of dead forms.
 He speaks of cups clean on the outside but polluted within,
  and of white-washed sepulchers.
 He dares to enter God's house
  and unmask the hypocrisy there.
 He declares that he is the new Moses,
  empowered to interpret the sacred law.
 He does all these things in the name
  and at the command of One
   he presumes to call his Father, and yet . . .

All: This man eats and drinks with sinners.

 And finally, on the night when he will be handed over,
  knowing who his betrayer is,
   His invitation to share the table with him
    on this most holy night
     is without reserve.

 "How I have longed to eat this Passover with you
  before my death."

Truly . . . *(together)* this man eats and drinks with sinners.

And so he does the new thing.

He takes the bread on the table before them,
 and giving thanks to the one he calls Father, he says,
  "Take this,
   all of you.

Eat it.
It is my body,
    being handed over for you."
And then he takes a cup of wine.
He says,
"Drink of this cup,
    all of you.
It is my blood,
    to be poured out as an irrevocable covenant
      with you
      and with all,
    so that the sins of all might be taken away.
You do these things
    and you will become my body.
Greater things than I have done you will do."

With full awareness of who we are, let us bless our God:

(Acclamation.)

We do what he commanded us to do,
    and in all our sinfulness
we are joined to him
    in his entry into death,
    his resurrection to new life,
    and the pouring out of his Spirit.

We pray that his Spirit may labor over this food and drink,
    that it may draw us ever more deeply
      into union with Jesus
      and his unbounded love.

In the power of that Spirit
we pray first for all those joined with us
    in the same faith around our earth.

We pray that the holy church may not be afraid
> to confess its sinfulness
> and so give glory to his power of forgiveness.

We pray that the church may become an ever clearer sign
> of God's compassion;
> that we may become reconcilers
> as we have been reconciled.

We pray that all the artificial barriers
> that keep people from sharing at this table
> may be removed.

That we may welcome with us at the table
> the straight and the gay;
> the single and the married and the divorced;
> those secure in their faith
> and those hanging on to it by a thread;
> those who have been abused
> and those who have abused.

That we may see in addicts
> our own petty addictions

and in saints
> our own potential
> for revealing the face of God.

We know that this table extends beyond the limits of our bodies.
> And so we find ourselves already at the table
> with those who have gone before us
> and taken their places at the other end of the table,
> beyond the transformation we call death,
> and with those who are not here yet
> who will be entrusted to our care for a brief moment.

We remember and celebrate their presence with us this night. *(Pause)*

We pray for the day
> when we will finally be fully one with them,

when the body of the Lord
>> will come to full consciousness of itself.

We make this prayer with the one
>> who chose to eat and drink with us at this table,
>>> Jesus the anointed of God.
For it is through him
>> and with him
>> and in him
that all glory and honor are yours, Eternal Creator,
in the unity of the Holy Spirit, now and forever. Amen.

READING
(For departure from the table.)

When Judas had gone out, Jesus said: Now the Son of Man is glorified, and in him God is glorified. My children, for a little while longer I am with you; then you will look for me, and I tell you now, where I am going you cannot come. I give you a new commandment: love one another; as I have loved you, so you are to love one another *(John 13:31-34)*.

Set your troubled hearts at rest. Trust in God always; trust in me. There are many dwelling places in my Father's house; I am going there on purpose to prepare a place for you. And if I go and prepare a place for you, I shall come again and receive you to myself, so that where I am you may be also *(John 14:1-3)*.

The word you hear is not mine; it is the word of the Father who sent me. I have told you all this while I am still here with you; but your Advocate, the Holy Spirit whom the Father will send in my name, will teach you everything, and will call to mind all that I have told you *(John 14:10, 24-26)*.

Peace is my parting gift to you, my own peace, such as the world cannot give. Set your troubled hearts at rest, and banish your fears. . . .
I shall not talk much longer with you, for the prince of this world approaches. He has no rights over me, but the world must be shown that I love the Father, and do exactly as he commands; so up, let us go forward! . . . In the world you will have trouble. But courage!
The victory is mine; I have conquered the world *(John 14:27, 30-31; 16:33)*.

After these words, Jesus went out with his disciples, and crossed the Kedron ravine *(John 18:1)*.

A Blessing of New Fire

Left to ourselves
> we can only huddle in our loneliness and isolation,
> > shivering against the darkness of unending night.

But your love, O God,
> would not allow us to remain cold and unfeeling.
> > You created fire to give us warmth and light
> > and energy and passion.

When we wandered in exile in the desert
> your fire took the form of a pillar,
> guiding us and giving us direction.

And when Jesus had completed your work
> and handed it all into your hands,
> > you sent your Spirit to hover in the form of fire
> > over the body of the infant church.

Tonight we ask you to bless the new fire we light in his name.
> Jesus declared that he was on fire with passion
> > until his baptism should be fulfilled.

So do we pray that this new fie may be but a small sign
> of the fire you will enkindle within each of us,
> > so that our lives may glow
> > with the compassion he revealed
> > and touch the hearts of all we meet,
> until at last he lays the whole of this creation at your feet
> > in adoration.
> For you are Lord for ever and ever. Amen.

A BLESSING OF WATER

Creator God, all of our beginnings are from water.
> The water from which all life slithered
>> onto the beaches of the land,
> and the comforting water of our mothers' wombs.

Since time began water has lapped the shores
> and tumbled over countless falls in breath-taking beauty;
>> it has glistened in the rainbow
>>> and quivered like a living pearl
>>>> on the edge of a leaf.

At the beginning of it all
> your Spirit hovered over restless, heaving water
>> and called forth life.

You taught us through a flood just who we are.
> When enemies pursued us and threatened to destroy us,
>> the waters became for us a protective shield of life,
>>> but for our enemies an unforgiving grave.

And finally, when Jesus took his place in the line before the Baptist
> and revealed his complete solidarity with us sinners
>> by submitting to his own baptism,
>>> you called him "beloved",
>>>> the one in whom you were well pleased.

And so this night we ask you to hover once more over this water
> which will seal our re-commitment.

> May it make us ever more trusting in your commitment to us;
>> may it give us warmth and passion and courage
>>> to proclaim to all your glory;
> and may it embolden us to do the works of justice and integrity
>> which Jesus promised we would do,
>>> as we become ever more like him
>>>> who is Lord for ever and ever. Amen.

Easter Sunday

A Baptismal Re-commitment

On the day each of us was baptized the gathered community used
water to join us to the mystery of Jesus and his baptism. Today
we will be sprinkled once again as a sign that we enter into a new
commitment, one never made before. In the year to come we will
confront a new world with new situations and new challenges, but our
God promises us new strength and new protection and new creativity
to face this future. And so I invite you:

In a world where profit rules,
>   where the categories of race and class and sex
>>   blot out the uniqueness of individual persons:

>   Do you pledge yourself
>   to struggle against oppression of every kind,
>   to recognize and promote the precious dignity
>>   of each of God's creatures?

In a world in which hatred and violence
>   are in the very air we breathe:

>   Do you pledge yourself
>   to work untiringly for genuine communion
>>   and solidarity
>>   among all people?

In a world in which the goods of science and technology,
>   of wealth and political power,
>>   are distorted into idols
>>   that disfigure the face of the living God in creation:

Do you pledge yourself
to use all the goods of this earth
only in dependence and gratitude to the God
    who gives life and being and holiness
        to everything in this creation?

Then I proclaim that we are "church",
    the newly gathered body of the risen Christ,
        empowered by his Spirit to confess the glory of our God.

BLESSING PRAYER

We wait one more time
    for the fullness of the resurrection, Lord.

And as we wait
    we join in the meal you have invited us to share.

The elements are simple:
    a loaf of bread,
    a cup of wine,
    the faith you have inspired in us,
    our feeble human bodies and spirits,
    and the story and the promise
        which hold it all together.

We recall all the signs of your fidelity
    down through the ages
        until the coming of Jesus the anointed one.

And we sing our oneness with all the heavenly hosts
    in the words of the prophet:

Holy, holy, holy Lord, God of power and might.
Heaven and earth are full of your glory.
Hosanna in the highest.
Blessed is he who comes in the name of the Lord.
Hosanna in the highest.

Then we re-tell the story.

We recall who is this Jesus with whom we dine:
    "I am the resurrection and the life."

All: I am the resurrection and the life.

And then we do what he did,
because he has told us to do so.
We take bread and we remember his promise:
    "This is my body, given for you."
And the cup, as he said:
    "And this cup is the new covenant in my blood;
        as often as you do these things, remember me,
           for I am with you
               till the end of time."

In great joy we remember him.

All: I am the resurrection and the life.

And in the power of the Spirit
    which transforms these gifts
    and is poured out upon us,
        we pray as one gathered people.

We pray that we may know the total gratuity of your gifts;
that we may not cling to what brings us only death,
not fear the new forms of life you desire to give us.

All: I am the resurrection and the life.

We pray that this food and drink will increase our sensitivities
so that we may find him in the most unexpected places:
> in defeat
> and powerlessness
> and weakness
> and death.

All: I am the resurrection and the life.

We pray that our Lenten watchfulness and waiting will continue
> even as we rejoice in the finality of his continued presence
> > among us.

All: I am the resurrection and the life.

And we pray that our eating and drinking
> will keep us joined to the host of the holy ones
> > who draw us forward to a final, eternal banquet
> > > with you,
> > > our welcoming God.

Through him
> who is Resurrection
and with him
> who is Life,
and in him
> who is our Way,
> > all glory and honor be yours
> > for ever and ever.
> > Amen.

23. FROM FRAGMENTATION TO UNITY

HOLY THURSDAY

(Replace the dated events in the text with current events.)

Whenever we come together for blessing, for eucharist, we are seeking wholeness. An instinct in the deepest recesses of our souls whispers to us that we are incomplete and isolated. It speaks of loss and fragmentation. This was not the way we were made, the way we were meant to be. Splintering is unnatural.

And so we gather. During these days we will dig into our roots and search out faint memories of old unities. We will join the pilgrimage of an ancient people called "the people of the way." We will dine by the wayside with the very One who *is* the Way. But first we must face our brokenness.

Reader 1: This year the age-old song of isolation rings in our ears perhaps more loudly than ever. In a land we couldn't name a few years ago — Bosnia — we have had to make up one more new expression to try to say what should not be able even to be imagined. "Ethnic cleansing." Ethnic *what?* Cleansing? Are we to believe that those who are flesh of our flesh and bone of our bone, the glory of the living God, are some sort of filthy muck into which we had fallen? So much dirt to be scraped away? Can human brothers and sisters be so focused on their own survival as to see one another like that?

Reader 2: Then in Israel, and in Ireland, our fragile hope that perhaps — just maybe, this time — the absurd response of violence might be seen for all its foolishness, is shattered once again. Same old, same old. The dirge goes on, while in our own land the chorus of isolation swells. "Keep the aliens out; build bigger fences!" "Save 'our' jobs and let the rest of the world fend for themselves." And meanwhile, as if there weren't enough already, we have to create a new category of crimes: "hate crimes."

Presider:
We each stand on such very small pieces of turf. The pieces have edges and the slightest slope could get slippery. Even the little we possess becomes the object of fierce protection. Up go the fences, and all the paraphernalia we need to shore them up. How painful the risk of reaching over from my plot to yours, to seek common ground. *(Pause.)* And yet we need to remind ourselves that it also part of our story that people do try — and sometimes succeed.

Reader 1: From every corner of our globe they came; by every means imaginable and at incredible costs. They came from homelands where they might not have been allowed to speak to one another. The women of the world. One body in Beijing. Communicating across barriers of custom and language and ideology all but impossible to scale. In the search for common ground.

Reader 2: And even the men came together. Men of color. Descendants of men and women once violently wrenched from their homelands and villages. Several hundred thousand they came, these

African-Americans. To the capital of the country which had enslaved them. To do a simple thing: to proclaim their dignity and their pride at being who they are — and to confess their embarrassment at what they had failed to be. And then a far more difficult thing: to commit themselves to begin again.

Presider:
And these efforts continue to bear fruit: women's groups meeting all around the world, African-American males creating neighborhood youth groups and groups to help fathers assume responsibility for their children. Just as earlier efforts to build common ground have continued to bear fruit. Call to Action. And the small band of women who set out in 1944 to found the holy place of Grailville. Let us thank our God for these signs of the presence of God's Spirit in the human effort to connect.

(A song of praise and thanksgiving; not jubilant but gentle thankfulness.)

So, this is who we are. Slivers of a fractured mirror; broken, yet still empowered to reflect, however poorly, the image of the living God. Let us sit quietly with our fragmentation, and our fear; our need and thirst for wholeness, and the inertia of old patterns we have allowed to direct us and deflect us from the way. From him who is the Way.

(Pause.)

I invite you now to turn to one person near you and share together your own experience of isolation and fragmentation. What is the most difficult bridge for me to cross? Who is the hardest to love? What patch of earth do I cling to, what ground am I unable to share? What fear blocks me? Then after a little while we will be called gently back to silence and we will listen to how our sisters and brothers in the early church found the key to unlock division.

(After the period of sharing.)

We find ourselves seated once more in the midst of brothers and sisters of a much earlier era, some of whom could actually have experienced the risen Lord, and we hear what is being said about their assemblies.

Reader 1: I have been told, my sisters and brothers, that there are quarrels among you. What I mean is this: each of you is saying, "I am Paul's man" or "I am for Apollos"; "I follow Cephas", or "I am Christ's." Surely Christ has not been divided among you! Was it Paul who was crucified for you? Was it in the name of Paul that you were baptized? Christ did not send me, Paul, to baptize, but to proclaim the Gospel; and to do it without relying on the language of worldly wisdom, so that the fact of Christ on his cross might have its full weight. This doctrine of the cross is sheer folly for those on their way to ruin, but for us who are on the way to salvation it is the power of God *(1 Corinthians 1:11-17).*

Reader 2: Scripture says, "I will destroy the wisdom of the wise, and bring to nothingness the cleverness of the clever." Where is your wise woman now, your man of learning, or your subtle debater — limited, all of them to this passing age? God has made the wisdom of this world look foolish . . . . The world failed to find God by its wisdom, and God chose to save those who have faith by the folly of the Gospel. Jews call for miracles, Greeks look for wisdom; but we proclaim Christ — yes, Christ nailed to the cross; and though this is a stumbling-block to Jews and folly to Greeks, yet to those who have heard his call, Jews and Greeks alike he is the power of God and the wisdom of God *(1 Corinthians 1:18-24).*

Presider:
I resolved that while I was with you I would think of nothing but Jesus

Christ — Christ nailed to the cross. I came before you weak, as I was then, nervous and shaking with fear. And yet I do speak words of wisdom to those who are ripe for it, not a wisdom belonging to this passing age, nor to any of its governing powers, which are declining to their end; I speak God's hidden wisdom, God's secret purpose framed from the very beginning to bring us to our full glory *(1 Corinthians 2:2-7).*

GREETING OF PEACE

The word has broken down all barriers and made us one people. And so before we join one another at the table of blessing let us greet one another in peace. But on this night on which Jesus is betrayed by a kiss, we are aware of the ambiguity of all symbols. So as we greet one another let us pray that the peace we extend is not simply good will, but the genuine peace of Christ — which is something much more profound. I wish you the peace of Christ.

(Participants greet one another in peace.)

Then let us learn how wisdom and peace and power act. Let us learn what alone can tear down the barrier between Jew and Greek, slave and free, woman and man; between our desire for wholeness and our fear of dissolution.

BLESSING PRAYER

Truly it is fitting,
> it is our privilege,
>> to bless and praise
>> and thank you,
>>> the all-holy One,
> especially for the ways you reveal to us
>> the saving mystery of your wisdom and power.

We raised a tower to the vault of heaven,
>   trying to make ourselves into gods;
>   and you showed us our real state
>   by scattering us across the face of the earth
>   in a confusion of tongues and voices
>   so we might learn the cost of genuine communion.

All: Your folly is wiser than our wisdom,
>   your weakness stronger than our strength.

We tried to save ourselves through weapons
>   and horses
>   and alliances
>   with the powers of this world;
>   and you revealed your tender compassion
>   and saving power
>   in the midst of our exile
>   and in the face of our complaining.

All: Your folly is wiser than our wisdom,
>   your weakness stronger than our strength.

You gave us a covenant as a mark of your special care,
>   and we turned it into an arrogant boast
>   and a way of excluding
>   and denigrating others;
>   you gave us the law as a path to blessedness,
>   and we made it into an idol
>   that stifled the freedom of your Spirit.

All: Your folly is wiser than our wisdom,
>   your weakness stronger than our strength.

Because we did not know you
>   — or ourselves —

we kept looking for signs and wonders;
we rejected your prophets
>>because their ideas of peace were costly.
And you gave us the most unlikely sign:
>>a young woman from a back-water village,
>>misunderstood by her husband,
>>the object of suspicion,
>>compelled to bear her child in a wayside shelter.

On such terms your Word became flesh. Indeed:

All: Your folly is wiser than our wisdom,
>>your weakness stronger than our strength.

In the face of this foolish wisdom,
>>confronted by this totally vulnerable power,
>>we can only bow our heads and join the prophet
>>>in the acknowledgment of your utter holiness:

>>>Holy, holy, holy Lord, God of power and might.
>>>Heaven and earth are full of your glory.
>>>Hosanna in the highest.
>>>Blessed is he who comes in the name of the Lord.
>>>Hosanna in the highest.

And so Jesus came among us.

And when his own time came,
>>he stood in front of the wilderness preacher
>>>and asked for baptism.

He let himself be led by the Spirit
>>into the desert,
>>>where he confronted the seduction of the tempter
>>>and submitted to your way;

proclaiming himself one with you
        the Holy One,
he sat and ate with the outcasts,
        the unclean,
        and the agents of foreign oppressors;
he fulfilled the law
        more radically than the letter ever could;
and with the courage of his own integrity
and trust in your total fidelity
        he went forward
                step by step
        toward Jerusalem
                where he knew the enemy awaited him.

All: Your folly is wiser than our wisdom,
        your weakness stronger than our strength.

Then at last,
        after letting himself be betrayed
                by one he called friend,
        he gave the final revelation
                of true wisdom and power,
                uniting all that was broken and fragmented in this world
                        in his own flesh broken,
                        his blood poured out.

He took the bread and wine from the table;
he blessed you for your faithfulness to the covenant;
and he said to his disciples,
        "Take this and eat it;
                it is my body broken for you.
        And drink from this cup of my blood;
                it is the new covenant,
                for you
                and everyone.

Whenever you do these things
　　　you will be proclaiming my death
　　　until I come again."

(Acclamation.)

And so as we remember
　　　who he was
　　　and how he lived
　　　and how he passed through death
　　　　　to the fullness of life,
we pray that his Spirit may be poured out upon us
　　　through our sharing in these gifts.

We pray that in some small way we,
　　　his gathered community,
may be led to a deeper realization
　　　that if we are to save our lives
　　　we must lose them.

All: Your folly is wiser than our wisdom,
　　　your weakness stronger than our strength.

We pray that we may come to know
　　　that genuine strength shines forth in vulnerability,
　　　that courage can reside within the center of fears confronted,
　　　　　that poverty can contain riches
　　　　　and even death be the entrance to life.

All: Your folly is wiser than our wisdom,
　　　your weakness stronger than our strength.

Through your Spirit
　　　help our church to let go of all the foolish substitutes
　　　that keep us from knowing the real source of our power;

the phony certitudes
and hollow displays
and sad recourse to intimidation.
Let us know your saving power
where you have always told us it would be found:
by identification with the orphan
and the widow
and the alien in the land.

We pray this night with all the holy ones gone before us —
every one of them broken—
who have revealed to us your wisdom
and your power
to touch
and heal
and reconcile.

(Pause.)

They are one already with us
though our eyes are shielded from such a powerful light.

One day our oneness will be revealed
when we dine in the fullness of the kingdom
at the table with Jesus the Christ.

It is through him
and in him
and with him
that all glory and honor are yours, Creator God,
through the unity of the Holy Spirit,
now and forever. Amen.

After the Meal

Presider:
His purpose in dying for all was that all, while still in life, should cease to live for themselves, and should live for him who for their sake died and was raised to life. With us therefore worldly standards have ceased to count in our estimate of any one; even if they counted in our understanding of Christ, they do so now no longer. When anyone is united to Christ, there is a new world; the old order has gone, and a new order has already begun *(2 Corinthians 5:15-17)*.

Honor and dishonor, praise and blame, are our lot alike; we are the impostors who speak the truth; the unknown ones whom everybody knows; dying we still live on; disciplined by suffering, we are not done to death; in our sorrows we always have cause for joy; poor ourselves, we bring wealth to many; penniless, we own the world *(2 Corinthians 6:8-10)*.

A Baptismal Re-Commitment for Holy Saturday Night

We have stood with Jesus as he revealed the secret of true wisdom and power which can bring all things together into wholeness. We have stood by a new fire and prayed to be bathed in fresh, living waters. And so I ask you now at this new moment on our journey:

Will you try to see your world with the eye of God's wisdom,
        judging all things not by the standard of human success
        but by their contribution to the life of the whole creation?

Will you accept your own weakness
        and seek to understand it as the place
        where the loving power of our God may be revealed?

Will you try to open yourself up in compassion
        for those who are unaccepted in our society,
        offering them your own weak voice
        to name their dignity as God's children?

Will you accept the call to find yourself by losing yourself,
        by stretching out your hand to touch and heal the wounds
        of division and fragmentation in our world,
        by continuing to search out common ground with the other,
        even if it means losing the secure place
        on which you had staked your own identity?

Then allow yourselves to be blessed with the living water,
        the gift of our ever-faithful God.

EASTER SUNDAY

On Holy Thursday we gathered, conscious of the fragmentation of peoples around our globe, and of our own brokenness. We were seeking a new experience of wholeness, a wisdom that would enable us to confront our sense of human isolation with courage and to find in the heart of that confrontation the energy and strength to continue our Christian task of building bridges and breaking down walls, of reaching out our hands to our sisters and brothers.

We were offered a strange wisdom and a paradoxical strength: a broken figure on a criminal's cross. Life to be discovered in the act of giving it away; a self to be found in losing it.

Then through these three days we have been led back to our roots, where we discovered that it was not so strange after all, that it was actually an old story re-told many times in wave after wave down through the history of our people: God revealing fidelity and compassion in the guise of human failure and defeat.

And today we join at the same table, with the same host, and the full meaning of it all will be revealed to us once more. New life comes through total acceptance of the kind sovereignty of our God.

> And so, may the peace and the joy
> > and the strength of the Risen Christ
> > > be with you this Easter day!

> Our ever-faithful and compassionate God,
> > we bless and thank you this day above all others.
> In the face of our fear
> > you reveal your continued saving presence among us;
> in the face of our aloneness and separation
> > you join us together into one people, even one body.

Through the power of Jesus, the one you raised to new life,
>   you draw the whole of this cosmos into unity.
All glory be to you this day and all days
>   till time be no more. Amen.

BLESSING PRAYER

Our always-faithful God, it is ever fitting
>   that we bless and praise you
>   >   for your fidelity to your covenant,
>   >   your promise that you will always stand with us.

We looked for you in all the wrong places.

We substituted kings for you;
>   we placed our reliance on arms and chariots;
>   we thought that a magnificent temple
>   >   would be our assurance of your favor;
>   we made even the covenant into a one-way magic cloak
>   >   that would absolve us of our responsibility.

And all the while you were present to us
>   in forms we were too blind to decipher:
>   In clouds and fire.
>   >   You went before us.

All: You went before us.

And manna and deserts.

All: You went before us.

And pagan rulers and fields of dried bones.

All: You went before us.

And when we were prepared to encounter you in thunderbolts,
　　you touched our faces with the faintest of breezes.

All: You went before us.

　　And finally it was not enough for you
　　　　to go before us.
　　You entered our midst,
　　　　to become one of us
　　　　　　as the child of a very ordinary young Jewish maid.

We praise you for your foolish wisdom,
　　your inconceivably vulnerable strength,
　　　　as we sing with the prophet:

　　　　Holy, holy, holy Lord, God of power and might.
　　　　Heaven and earth are full of your glory.
　　　　Hosanna in the highest.
　　　　Blessed is he who comes in the name of the Lord.
　　　　Hosanna in the highest.

　　And so you pitched your tent
　　　　within our flesh,
　　　　in a man from Nazareth, Jesus.
　　In him you walked beside us.

You set yourself within a family
　　like ours;
　　a family that continually misunderstood you
　　　　and your plan,
　　　　that tried to restrain your zeal
　　　　　　and your madness.
　　You walked beside us.

All: You walked beside us.

You drew to yourself men
>who were ignorant
>and obtuse
>and petty
>and jealous;
you turned upside down the distorted values
>of religious leaders.

All: You walked beside us.

You found dignity and value in those scorned and rejected:
>Samaritans and lepers and children,
>tax gatherers and prostitutes.

All: You walked beside us.

And at last, in the body of Jesus
you identified yourself
>with all our sufferings.
You sat at table with us
>and said you longed to eat this meal
>>with us.
You washed our feet and told us
>there is true wisdom and genuine power to be found
>>if we would wash one another's feet.

Then Jesus took his place with us forever.

He took the bread lying on the table
and he blessed you for your faithfulness.
>And he did the new thing:
>he broke the bread
>and gave it to his disciples
>>and to us,
with the words:

"Take this and eat it.
This is my body.
It is being broken and given for you."

And so, too, he took the cup of wine
and gave it to them, saying,
        "Drink of this cup, all of you.
        It is the new covenant in my blood,
                spilled for all.
        Do these same things yourselves when you gather,
                to celebrate my death
                        until I come again."

(Acclamation.)

And so we proclaim his earthly life among us,
his passage through death to a new risen life;
and in the power of his Spirit
        poured out on us this day
we are joined as his single body,
        made whole once more.

We believe that we,
        your church
        gathered around the world
        in so many nations
        and peoples
        and cultures,
are empowered to do the deeds which bind up
        what has been fractured
        and broken,
for you go before us.

All: For you go before us.

Men and women like us will stand before tribunals
and speak for the forgotten,
> for pariahs
> and refugees
> and the innocent.

All: For you go before us.

Peace-makers will protest violence
and artists will reveal the holiness of all creation
and children will teach us wisdom through their fragility.

All: For you go before us.

We walk together with the countless throng of those
> who have learned wisdom and strength
by joining Jesus in his passage,
> women and men of every land and nation
>> risen and awaiting our fulfillment.

And so will the mystery continue,
> of your emptying yourself,
> our compassionate God,
until you lead us to that perfect banquet
> where we will join with them in singing your praises,
>> finally made whole in the body of the Risen One.

Through him
and with him
and in him
all glory and honor are yours, Creator God,
in the unity of the Holy Spirit, now and forever. Amen.

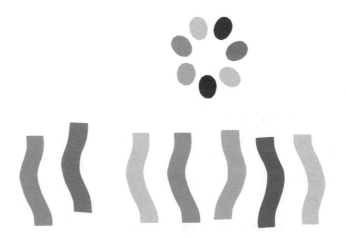

24. THE GOD WHO GOES BEFORE US

OPENING PRAYER

Creator God, you are the God of life, the God of all the living.
You bless us with the life of rich food and refreshing drink;
the life of beauty in all the lovely images of this creation;
the life of communion with brothers and sisters
    who share this planet with us.
In Jesus you have shown us
    that even death cannot strangle this life,
    that it is a spring welling up
        into forms we cannot imagine,
        into eternal joy and blessing.
As you raised up Jesus and made him our pledge of completion,
    continue your work in us this day and every day
    until your pledge is fully redeemed
and we are at last one with Jesus and all your holy people,
    sharing his life forever.
We ask this in his name
    who has become the first-born from the dead,
        Jesus Christ,
        our Lord and brother. Amen.

BLESSING PRAYER

Beyond all doubt
　　　it is right,
　　　and fitting,
　　　and the fullest expression of who we are,
that we should always praise and bless your name.

For you are the source of our life
and without you we vanish into nothingness.

But out of all our days
it is on this day above all
　　　that our very being must cry out
　　　　　in joyful benediction.

For it is today that you renew us
and give us new hope
　　　by calling Jesus forth from the tomb
　　　and crowning him as the Christ,
　　　　　the fullness of all life.

It was an old tale,
for again and again
　　　you had brought life out of our deaths of sin
　　　　　and fear
　　　　　and unbelief.

We rebelled in the garden,
trying to snatch the gift of life from you,
and even as you were compelled to cast us out on our own,
you promised that the seed of the woman would prevail.
You were the living one, going before us on our way.

All: You were the living one, going before us on our way.

We languished in slavery,
and you led us forth from our captivity.

All: You were the living one, going before us on our way.

We were dazed with the cost of it all in the desert,
and you found yet another way to feed us
for the way still ahead of us.

All: You were the living one, going before us on our way.

You took the form of a cloud by day
and a pillar of fire by night,
to mark out our path for us.

All: You were the living one, going before us on our way.

When the pagan conquerors swarmed over our country
and defiled even the sacred place of the Holy of Holies,
you came to us
through an even more holy temple,
the womb of Mary.

All: You were the living one, going before us on our way.

And so on this most special day
we marvel at all these signs
of the irrepressibility of your care for us.

We join the body of the blessed
in chanting the awe that Isaiah felt
in your sacred presence:

Holy, holy, holy Lord, God of power and might.
Heaven and earth are full of your glory.
Hosanna in the highest.
Blessed is he who comes in the name of the Lord.
Hosanna in the highest.

And then the story of your care reached its fullness
    in the human flesh of Jesus.
Again and again in his earthly mission
    he brought new life from old deaths.
He was the living one, going before us on our way.

All: He was the living one, going before us on our way.

He touched the ears of the deaf
    and the tongue of the dumb
    and the body of a lifeless young man,
and he called forth newness and power in them.

All: He was the living one, going before us on our way.

He stripped away
    the strangling forms of religious hypocrisy
      and called whited sepulchers
        to become new living temples.

All: He was the living one, going before us on our way.

He translated images
    that had become trivialized
    and domesticated,
and breathed the fire of his Spirit into them
    so that they might once more be revealed
    as the breathing word of the living God.

All: He was the living one, going before us on our way.

And then he showed us
        the radical power of the life you offer us,
                by pouring it out,
                in faithful response to you.

But before he entered upon his death,
he offered himself to us
        as food and drink.

As we recall the story,
we call upon his Spirit
        to bless the food and drink before us,
                that it might become his life for us.

At the holy supper of his people,
he rejoiced to be with them,
        even as his betrayer reclined with him.
He ate their holy meal
        and sang the ancient songs of his people.

And then,
        without warning,
he fulfilled the promise he had shared
        long before they could comprehend its meaning.

He took some bread from the table.
He blessed you,
        the Source of his own life.
And breaking it
        he gave it to them with the words,
                "Here is my body.
                Take it and eat it.
                I am giving it over for you."

And then he took a cup of wine.
Blessing you again,
>he offered it to them, saying,
>>"Here is the cup of my blood.
>>It seals a new covenant,
>>>a commitment which cannot be broken.
>>I will pour it out in my death
>>>but it will become in you
>>>>a fountain of eternal life.

>When you gather as my people,
>>remember me
>>and do these same things."

(Acclamation.)

In the power of his Spirit
we re-live his time among us,
>his passage through death to new life,
>and the gift of his life-giving Spirit
>>shaping us as his body in the world.
His Spirit is the living one, going before us on our way.

All: His Spirit is the living one, going before us on our way.

We join with the whole family of the faith
>gathered around the globe,
>praying for the gifts he has promised.

We pray that we,
>his people,
may experience in our very bones
>the call to be compassion,
>to be justice,
>to be peace in this world.

All: His Spirit is the living one, going before us on our way.

We pray that we may know
how to make ourselves into food
for the nourishment of our brothers and sisters,
into drink
that brings them joy,
into companionship
that can lighten their steps
and help them to dance in your presence.

All: His Spirit is the living one, going before us on our way.

We pray in solidarity with the leaders you give us,
with the pope,
and our bishop,
and all men and women around the earth
who keep the search for you alive
in our world.

We know that the life we share on this earth
is not ours alone.
That we hold it in common
with the rest of his body and ours,
with all those who have gone before us on the journey
and accompany us on each step of our path.

We pray for their support
and their wisdom
even as we praise you
for their life-giving example.
One day we will know the fullness of life
with them
at that richer banquet in your kingdom,
as Jesus hands it all back to you.

For it is through him
> and with him
> and in him,
> that all glory and honor are yours, Eternal Creator,
> in the unity of the Holy Spirit,
>> now and forever. Amen.

25. A Transforming God

Introduction to the Ritual of Light

We prepare ourselves now to hear the Lord's word to us
this night. At our places at table we each have an unlit candle. It
represents our individual self and our need for the fire of God's
wisdom to light our way through the darkness and enflame in us a
passion for deeper transformation.

For a moment pray quietly out of that desire in yourself.

Then I will lead members at our table in going to the center to receive
the light of Christ which declares that God is with us. Other tables
follow in clockwise manner until we each have a lighted candle at our
place. As we light our candles the choir will lead us in singing the Fire
Song. As we each light our candle we are invited to say our name
quietly as a sign of our will to be fully present to the Lord's word
during these holy days. Be mindful of your companions at your table;
one or other may ask you to help them by taking their candle up and
lighting it for them.

INTRODUCTION TO THE SCRIPTURE READINGS

We come to hear the Lord's word and share in the mystery of Jesus
tonight as a people in need, but also as a people of hope.

Our need is all too evident. We watch helplessly as men in Kosovo
are brutally killed and their wives and children driven from their
homes into refugee camps, with little hope of ever returning home.
In our name weapons of terrible destruction are rained upon our
earth, by men and women who genuinely and desperately desire to
put an end to the slaughter of innocent people. On our own streets
African-Americans live in fear of those who are pledged to protect
them. As a people we enjoy wealth our ancestors could scarcely dream
of, and still we cannot summon the will to release the people of poor
countries from the crushing burden of their debt.

Each of us has stood helplessly by as relationships among people
we love have crumbled and deteriorated. We have longed for
reconciliations and have had to confront our inability to bring them
about.

We have been compelled by hard experience to recognize the unreality
of our utopian expectations, in our society and in our church. We
have become afraid to dream; for we know now how painful is the
death of a dream. We know we can't go back but so often we seem to
be unable to see the way forward.

And what is our hope? That the God who has promised to be with
us will work within us to transform us and light a path before us —
wherever that path is to take us.

Transformation is an attractive word. It speaks of new energies and
new clarities and new forms of wholeness beyond the capacity of our
feeble imaginations. But it also speaks of letting go, and that is the
hard part. What is to be transformed must be wrenched free from old

attachments, from ways of looking that were not ways of seeing, from ways of hearing that were not ways of listening, from ways of sympathizing that were not ways of caring. From identifications that have become unhealthy dependencies, and illusions that masqueraded as dreams.

During these days we take our places at the center of the one great transformation that alone can make sense of all the others, the transformation of Jesus of Nazareth into the Christ of the cosmos. We will try once again to learn, to appreciate what that transformation meant for Jesus so that we can appreciate what it must mean for us.

But above all we want not merely to listen but more to stand within that mystery, to receive it and let it work within us. For the same God who worked then in Jesus of Nazareth works now in us; the God who dreamed the Christ of the cosmos wills to make us more fully members of that Christ — if we can allow it to happen. We listen to the word.

First Reading: 1 Corinthians 2:1-13,16

When I came to you, sisters and brothers, proclaiming the mystery of God, I did not come with sublimity of words or of wisdom. For I resolved to know nothing while was with you except Jesus Christ, and him crucified. I came to you in weakness and fear and much trembling, and my message and my proclamation were not with persuasive wisdom, but with a demonstration of spirit and power, so that your faith might rest not on human wisdom but on the power of God.

Yet we do speak a wisdom to those who are mature, but not a wisdom of this age, nor of the rulers of this age who are passing away. Rather we speak of God's wisdom, mysterious, hidden, which God predetermined before the ages for our glory, and which none of the rulers of this age knew for, if they had known it, they would not have crucified the Lord of glory. But as it is written: "What eye has not seen, and ear has not heard, and what has not entered the human heart, what God has prepared for the who love God," this God has revealed to us through the Spirit.

For the Spirit scrutinizes everything, even the depths of God. Among human beings, who knows what pertains to a person except the spirit of the person that is within? Similarly, no one knows what pertains to God except the Spirit of God. We have not received the spirit of the world but the Spirit that is from God, so that we may understand the things freely given by God. And we speak about them not with words taught by human wisdom, but with words taught by the Spirit. . . . We have the mind of Christ.

(Cantors sing: "Christus factus est".)

Second Reading: John 13: 1-17

Before the feast of Passover, Jesus knew that his hour had come to pass from this world to the Father. He loved his own in the world and he loved them to the end. The devil had already induced Judas, son of Simon, to hand him over. So, during supper, fully aware that the Father had put everything into his power and that he had come from God and was returning to God, he rose from supper and took off his outer garments. He took a towel and tied it around his waist. Then he poured water into a bowl and began to wash the disciples' feet and dry them with the towel around his waist. He came to Simon Peter, who said to him, "Master, are you going to wash my feet?" Jesus answered and said to him, "What I am doing, you do not understand now, but you will understand later." Peter said to him, "You will never wash my feet." Jesus answered him, "Unless I wash you, you will have no inheritance with me." Simon Peter said to him, "Master, then not only my feet, but my hands and head as well." Jesus said to him, "Those who have bathed have no need except to have their feet washed, for they are clean all over; so you are clean, but not all." For he knew who would betray him; for this reason, he said, "Not all of you are clean."

So when he had washed their feet and put his garments back on and reclined at table again, he said to them, "Do you realize what I have done for you? You call me 'teacher' and 'master', and rightly so, for indeed I am. If I, therefore, the master and teacher, have washed your feet, you ought to wash one another's feet. I have given you a model to follow, so that as I have done for you, you should also do."

INSTRUCTIONS FOR TABLE SHARING

Each of us has the light of the Holy Spirit. I invite you now to share that light, that experience, that wisdom, with those at your table.

> *(Where have you seen the mystery reveal itself,*
> *either in your own life or that of people around you?)*

> *(Where have you seen breakdown*
> *transformed into reconciliation?*
> *Forms of death become the surprising spring of new life?*
> *Failure become the discovery of new possibility?)*

> Tell your fellow pilgrims.

INSTRUCTIONS AT THE CONCLUSION OF THE SHARING

We have told each other our stories; we have become church. As a sign of our collective wisdom our candles will be gathered into one brilliant fire around Christ's light and we will join in eucharist with our sisters and brothers around the world.

BLESSING PRAYER

It could not be more fitting
      that we should praise you,
           God of all wisdom,
you who create
      and constantly transform
           this universe
                out of sheer delight.

When our ancestors were enslaved
and could see no way out of their oppression,
      you became a burning bush,
      a sacred fire.

In Moses you fascinated us — and terrified us.

You held out a future for us
and promised to show us a way.
Above all, you promised that you would walk beside us
      at every step along that way.
You made us your people
      and said you would be our God.
And down through the ages you have kept your word.

You came as fire and light and freedom —
      but always as surprise,
      in forms we could never have anticipated.
You came as a pagan king from Persia;
you came to us in a fiery furnace;
you came in the slingshot of a teenage shepherd;
and you came as a child in the womb of a young Jewish girl
      from a back-water village.

With that mighty cloud of witnesses

who have believed in your promise
> down through the ages
> and have been a source of light and wisdom to us,
>> we sing your praise in the words of Isaiah:

Holy, holy, holy Lord, God of power and might.
Heaven and earth are full of your glory.
Hosanna in the highest.
Blessed is he who comes in the name of the Lord.
Hosanna in the highest.

Above all,
> God of the burning bush,
we praise you for the mystery of your enfleshment
> in Jesus of Nazareth.

He walked our earth
> with men and women of our race
and called them not servants but friends.
May his Spirit live on in us.

All: May his Spirit live on in us.

He who was on fire till his baptism would be accomplished
> learned to wait for his hour.

All: May his Spirit live on in us.

He who shared your divine life
> learned the limits of our humanity:
> he wept at the loss of friends,
> and he anguished over those who were like sheep
>> without shepherds,
> and he endured within himself rage and frustration
>> over the hypocrisy of false leaders.

All: May his Spirit live on in us.

And he wept over the city he loved
       because it blinded itself to the time of its visitation.

All: May his Spirit live on in us.

Finally he had to face the full mystery to be revealed in him.
He shrunk with terror at the cup he was to drink.

Yet even in that hour he was mindful of his weak disciples.

He gave himself to them
       and to us
in a new and irrevocable commitment.

They were at a supper
       like ours.
He sang with them the songs of his people.
He gave them a new commandment,
       to love one another as he loved,
       even to laying down their lives.

And then
       at a single moment in history
          he did the most surprising thing.

He took the bread in front of them;
he offered it in blessing;
and he said,
       "Take this.
       All of you.
       Eat of it.
       It is my body, to be handed over for you."

And he took a cup of wine.
He had longed to drink of it with them.
And he said,
    "Share this cup among you.
        Drink from it, all of you.
        It is the cup of my blood,
        to be poured out in love for you.
    Whenever you gather as my people,
        you do these same things in memory of me."

(Acclamation: "We remember how you loved us . . .")

We do remember.
We celebrate his life among us.
We believe that his risen life came
    only through the mystery of his entry into death.
And we believe that his Spirit has been poured out upon us,
    to make us who were "no people" into "your people"
        in this world.

In the power of that Spirit
we are joined in prayer
    with our brothers and sisters in faith around our world.
May the fire of his Spirit transform our church.

All: May the fire of his Spirit transform our church.

May we not fear the cost of life born out of death.

All: May the fire of his Spirit transform our church.

May we show forth the works of genuine caring
    for our neighbors, flesh of our flesh,
        in their hour of need;

and may we raise our voices in non-violent protest
>   for those whose voices are stifled
>   by the powers of this world.

All: May the fire of his Spirit transform our church.

>   Show us that we are not alone in the face of those powers.
>   Join our prayer with all those
>   who believed in the promise
>   and did deeds of unimaginable courage
>   down through the centuries
>   and even within our own days.
>   Keep fresh in us
>   the hope that we will join with them one day
>   at an unending banquet in your kingdom.

>   We pray in Jesus' name.
>   For it is through him
>   and with him
>   and in him
>   that all honor and glory are yours, Eternal Creator,
>   in the unity of the Holy Spirit, now and forever. Amen.

INSTRUCTIONS AFTER THE OUR FATHER AND PEACE PRAYER

Our church has a long tradition of abstaining from a kiss of peace on Holy Thursday so that we may not forget how easily a kiss became a sign of betrayal — how costly the commitment to real peace might be. In that spirit I invite you simply to join hands with those at your table as the choir leads us in singing our peace.

Concluding Prayer

Our transforming God,
  we have stood in your presence this night
  in a humble profession of our weakness and need.
And once again you have offered us
  the food of hope and promise,
  the very life of Jesus-become-the Christ.
We will continue to walk in mystery with him
  in these coming days.
Give us the sensitivity
  to recognize that his Spirit walks with us,
  and to see the ways your transforming power
   is always at work in us
   and in the whole of your creation.

We ask this through Christ our Lord. Amen.

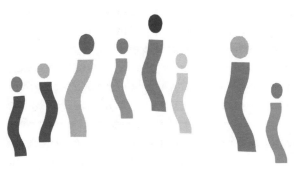

Afterword

Composing Your Own Blessing Prayers

It is my fond hope that the prayer texts in this work will provide spiritual nourishment for the personal and communal prayer of its readers. But my wise and helpful editor has suggested that it could be of even greater help if I were to reflect on the process by which the prayers came to be composed. I might by this means be able to draw out some of the principles of method to be discovered in the act of composing. Such a reflection might then support readers in the next stage of their response to the work: to use the present prayers not only for their worship but also as a springboard in composing their own unique prayers of blessing.

Hence this *Afterword*. It is an attempt to 'catch' and name what transpired in me as I labored over the choices of structure and word.

It must be said at the outset that the effort will be inherently unsatisfying, because the composition took place within the mystery of my own spirit Some words and images and concepts were ultimately chosen and committed to paper, of course, so some criteria must have been at work. Other words and images and concepts flashed on my mental screen, tugged at me for expression, and were either rejected, filed away for future contemplation, or simply evaporated as mysteriously as they had appeared. And — for sure — yet others never even made it that far, but tumble about still in the deepest caves of my spirit, as powerful as they are inaccessible — powerful perhaps precisely because of their inaccessibility. Who can comprehend the human heart?

Inadequately then, but in an effort to be of further service.

An Attitude and a Purpose

Before the execution, we need to consider the goal of the writing. The prayers were composed for a particular transitory community, at a particular moment in the life of their — our — world. But that community, for all its uniqueness, is itself presently inserted into, and making its mark upon, the great gathering which the Spirit of Jesus and the Father is constantly creating: the body of all those consciously joined to the continued life and worship offered by the Jesus of Nazareth who has become the Christ of the cosmos. The goal of the writing, however faithful or poor an expression it may be of the writer's own spirit, was simple and direct: to serve as a vehicle which would gather those separate individuals in common worship of God on that particular evening. The criterion of success was thus equally forthright: not the rhetorical elegance of the texts, nor even the passion of the writer, but simply — what deceptive simplicity! — whether the word written and proclaimed would help those participants to be for that brief moment a single worshiping body. A house church.

If the language of the liturgy does not evoke corporate prayer in its participants, what good is it? These are not, after all, just a collection of atomized individuals who happen to occupy the same space at the same time. They are already joined by invisible threads of conviction and aspiration; that single latent tapestry is crying for visibility and incarnation in our world. It is that drive that the words must support.

The simple clarity of purpose creates in its turn a different imperative for the one charged with the privilege and responsibility of generating the human medium. The "stuff" of the text must be born of prayer in the spirit of the one composing. What does the Psalmist say? "Deep calls to deep in the roar of your cataracts."

There are several components in the one goal. To try to express the action of the Spirit in one's own spirit. To offer the product of the writer's personal prayer to the gathered faithful as a service to their becoming a gathered church. To invite them into consciousness and celebration of who they really are as a people-within-the-People claimed by Jesus. Upon reflection, this is the only goal and attitude which makes the effort of any worth.

Principles of a Structure

As I indicated in my introduction, the process always began, not with the writer, but in the prayerful reflection of a small group charged with preparing the form for the common worship (in the case of the prayers in this book, it was a gathering of five or six women and myself). The planning group was itself enough of a community to be able to work at naming each one's personal experience of the God at work in their lives and worlds, and then to let that personal naming be, if not directly denied, at least diverted, modulated (almost beyond all recognition), or undercut by the stuttered effort of someone else's naming. It is hard enough work to find expression for the God at work in one's own spirit, focusing only on one's immediate life. How much more complex to try to name what the Holy One might be stirring within the collective spirit of a given community, when the scope of the reflection extends beyond the limits of their daily rounds to the workings of God in the city, the nation, the collection of nations, indeed in the very universe we inhabit?

We tried. We were frustrated. We fumbled. There were brief flashes of excitement, of possible insight. To be followed by long pauses of wondering if that was 'it' at all. Participants spoke of feelings and hunches and movements within them. They/we dredged up patches of memory; seemingly unconnected stories; ideas from a book that was still moving within them or a snatch of song occasioned by a passing comment. There were moments of humor and irony, boisterous and irreverent laughter — the children of God at home in the house of the Lord, free to play with things too sacred to be allowed to become sanctimonious.

What are we experiencing? And what is God about in all this swirling world of jumbled experiences — not "then", not last year, but today, now? If today you hear God's voice. And who does that make us? To what are we being called? These are not things easily captured.

And so we discover a principle which was not proclaimed ahead of the planning effort but embedded in the living process: community prayer emerges out of community reflection on experience — on the God at work in creation as the Spirit gives us to experience and name that working.

It is true, that the faithful who would eventually gather for this common worship could not be present, face to face, for the reflection from which the common prayer began; they were scattered across the land. But the worshiping community was already present in the trust extended to the small planning group, and then in the planning group's act of handing over the results of its reflection to the final wordsmith.

A further element of method bubbles up from the reflection. The members of the planning group (though membership varied from year to year) were without exception women steeped in the wealth of both the Hebrew and Christian scriptures. They were people who had experience with ritual drawn from many cultures, whose sure sense of the body that would be gathering for worship told them immediately that some proposed gesture, good enough in itself, would "fit" — or, by contrast, would come across as contrived or hokey. How might this community authentically express in their bodies things like estrangement or reconciliation, shame or liberation, depression or exuberant enjoyment of our God?

And so, two more principles emerge. One, that Christian prayer draws its best energies from the history of the people out of whom the present generation issues, from the scriptures. And two, that bodily ritual cannot be some foreign expression, however suited to another people, but must be solidly rooted in the ethos of this enculturated people. Not that it must be so practiced that it has become bland or risk-free. Precisely the opposite: if it is to evoke energy in this moment, it needs to contain some element of the untried. Sometimes the ritual gestures we invited people into were experienced as prayer, as authentic self-expression of the community's sense of itself; sometimes they were less so.

The Text Itself

It is easy to see that these prayers of blessing had as their springboard the officially recognized Eucharistic prayers of the Catholic tradition, the "canon" of the liturgy. As the desire for expressions that might be more spiritually evocative for this particular community grew, so did a certain sense of freedom to adapt and use new images and words to achieve what the standard forms were no longer able to achieve — for this body of the gathered faithful.

But the energy arising out of freedom was accompanied by a felt responsibility: to keep the emerging formulations grounded in the same faith experience from which the standard texts had themselves presumably been mined by some earlier generation of believers. Each prayer would attempt to evoke responses to what God seemed to be doing and revealing in a given Holy Week, but there was a common framework to keep each from spiraling off into any one of the many possible distortions of the meaning and mission of Jesus that have appeared across the centuries.

Upon reflection after the fact, the prayers are held together by a structure which successively highlights:

a) The origins of Jesus in the soil of creation and in the heritage of a unique people, at once secular and covenantal, in a story of salvific events culminating in the holy Cry of Isaiah;

b) Some events or aspects of his earthly story which shed special light on the common experience we are bringing to prayer at the moment;

c) The narrative of the holy meal which sums up the meaning of all his earthly existence, his laying down his life as the perfect sign of the love which is the kingship of the Father;

d) The link to the Spirit of Jesus disclosed in the subsequent life of the faithful community of God's people; and

e) The conscious recall of how the total body of God's people transcends the limits of earthly existence: the unity of the communion of holy ones across the ages.

A Word About Each

a) Creation and the People of Israel.

The God who works through the person and deeds of Jesus is the same God who is originally and continually at work in the creation of the universe. A Jesus who does not share with us all the potential as well as the limitation of finite embodiment is a gnostic idea, not the incarnate Word of God. So, too, a Jesus whose whole being does not come shaped by the events of God's working in the life, exile, release, and covenantal union of the Israelite people with the One he called "Abba" is a useless abstraction, a unenculturated cardboard cutout. Each of the prayers attempts to root our sense of Jesus in the reality of creation and the historical story of his origins.

b) The events of Jesus' own human life as received from the Christian community.

The covenantal relationship and attitude of Jesus comes to expression — and therefore can become accessible to us — only in the human events of his earthly life: in his interaction with the stuff of creation and the people whose earthly path intersects with his own. The Gospels and other writings of the New Testament may not indeed be a journalistic account of 'what really happened' but they tell — in the form of a genre unique to them, to be sure — the story of a human life. Our access to Jesus of Nazareth and hence to the Christ of the cosmos is ultimately only through that narrow door. Each of the prayers, after grounding the Jesus reality in creation and the people from whom he springs, attempts to evoke some realities in that story which might shed light on the present stuff in which we are being touched by God.

c) The narrative of the final meal.

The whole of the New Testament points to the centrality of that final meal at which Jesus summed up the meaning of his life and the offering of himself into death as the completion of his proclamation of the reign of God. It is in approaching the telling of this pivotal narrative that one feels perhaps the most reluctance to 'tamper with' the wording given to us across so many centuries. And yet the four evangelists themselves each found their own individual words to tell the same story. Each version gives a different subtle shading which holds a different facet up to the light while allowing other aspects to recede into the background; by substituting the power-filled account of Jesus washing the feet of the disciples John is free even to reveal what the event is about without reciting "the institution" itself. Similarly, in the variety of narrative in the canonical formulations the church implicitly tells us that there is no single "correct" way to communicate the event. So in each of the prayers in the book I felt free to surround the story with different elements that might mine a different truth or call for a different conversion in us. Apparently the one element one can ill afford to overlook is that in all accounts Jesus is being betrayed as he gives himself away.

d) The continued life of Jesus through the outpouring of the Spirit in the church.

The scriptures make clear that the Jesus story comes to completion only in the new form by which his new form of life, the resurrection, is made available to the community of believers down through the centuries to the present day. To pray to a Jesus who has gone off to some Norman Rockwell heaven is to distort the meaning of all that preceded the gathering of his community. Paul tells us that the Spirit of Jesus is praying within us right now, impelling us toward that unity whereby we become the organs of his continued life on this earth. The story of the church, with the glorious deeds of individual believers as well as the painful ways in which we cloud and hide and distort the revelation given to us in our Baptism, is one seamless narrative with the journey of Jesus of Nazareth. In each of the prayers in the book we are reminded of who this praying body of the faithful is, a continuation of the people continually being led through the rushing torrent on left and right to the "other side."

e) Continuity with those who go before us.

Finally, the story is inadequate if it does not disclose our oneness with the great cloud of witnesses imaged in Hebrews, if our painful experience of separation from those who gave us life and faith by the force of their own commitment is not transcended in the vision and hope of full reunion with them at the single table of the kingdom. Without that hope we are not the people we are called to be.

A Final Freedom

For many of the years in which these prayers were composed and proclaimed, for all their free departure from the canonical formulae, one clear tie to liturgical custom remained untouched. The prayers were written for proclamation by one person. The presider was, to be sure, speaking in the name of the community and serving the prayer of the community by calling the prayer within each participant into the circle of prayer of the whole body. Still only one voice actually voiced the prayer.

At a given moment the question arose: why not enable the whole body to voice its prayer? Why not, indeed?

And so in the later prayers of the collection the reader will have noted the emergence of a kind of antiphonal or responsory form. With the community's comfort at adapting and moving into new modes of expression we moved quite effortlessly into a new practice. The prayers began to be so composed that at certain points — without any practice or 'stage directions' — the presider would simply indicate with a slight gesture of the hand or through eye contact and the congregation would instinctively know that they were being invited to repeat the phrase or sentence that had just been spoken. For purposes of the present text, in which the message is being transmitted through the written word instead of present gesture, the places where such a congregational response is in order are so indicated.

Conclusion

Doubtless there were other criteria and principles at work in the effort to bring these images and ideas, these aspirations and convictions to expression. I have tried, however feebly, to name the process that gave rise to this body of prayers. It is my hope that you, our readers, will be able to shed light on other rich insights to be uncovered in the effort to write for your own communities. It is one body. We are all in this together.

George B. Wilson, S.J.
gbwilson@choice.net

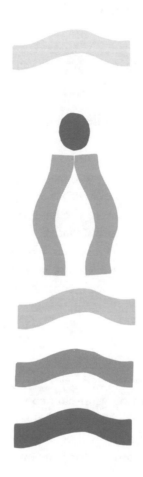